Magic and Moon Spells

The Ultimate Guide to Unlocking the Power of Natural Forces, the 8 Lunar Phases, Wicca, and Witchcraft

© Copyright 2021

This document is geared towards providing exact and reliable information regarding the topic and issue covered. The publication is sold with the idea that the publisher is not required to render accounting, officially permitted, or otherwise, qualified services. If advice is necessary, legal or professional, a practiced individual in the profession should be ordered from a Declaration of Principles which was accepted and approved equally by a Committee of the American Bar Association and a Committee of Publishers and Associations.

In no way is it legal to reproduce, duplicate, or transmit any part of this document in either electronic means or in printed format. Recording of this publication is strictly prohibited and any storage of this document is not allowed unless with written permission from the publisher. All rights reserved.

The information provided herein is stated to be truthful and consistent, in that any liability, in terms of inattention or otherwise, by any usage or abuse of any policies, processes, or directions contained within is the solitary and utter responsibility of the recipient reader. Under no circumstances will any legal responsibility or blame be held against the publisher for any reparation, damages, or monetary loss due to the information herein, either directly or indirectly.

Respective authors own all copyrights not held by the publisher.

The information herein is offered for informational purposes solely, and is universal as so. The presentation of the information is without contract or any type of guarantee assurance.

The trademarks that are used are without any consent, and the publication of the trademark is without permission or backing by the trademark owner. All trademarks and brands within this book are for clarifying purposes only and are owned by the owners themselves, not affiliated with this document.

Your Free Gift (only available for a limited time)

Thanks for getting this book! If you want to learn more about various spirituality topics, then join Mari Silva's community and get a free guided meditation MP3 for awakening your third eye. This guided meditation mp3 is designed to open and strengthen ones third eye so you can experience a higher state of consciousness. Simply visit the link below the image to get started.

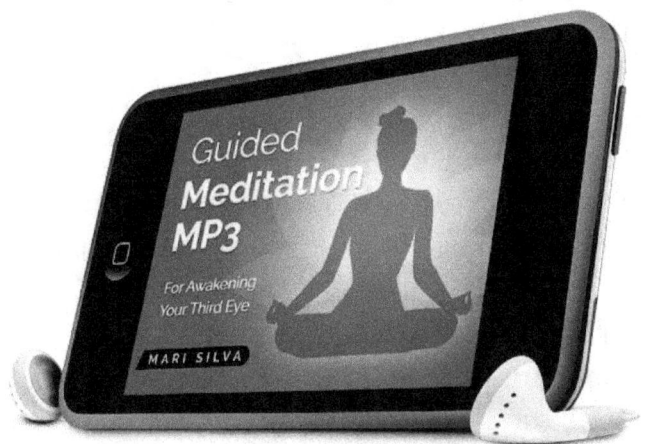

https://spiritualityspot.com/meditation

Contents

PART 1: MAGIC 1
INTRODUCTION 2
CHAPTER ONE: ACKNOWLEDGING THE MAGIC WITHIN 4
    The Goal of Magic 6
    A Rational Explanation of Magic 7
    Magic and NLP 9
    The Power is Within You 10
CHAPTER TWO: MAGICAL LAW: DO WHAT YOU WILL 14
    Discovering Your True Will: The Key to Transformation 14
    Dispelling the Myths Surrounding the Magical Law 18
CHAPTER THREE: MEDITATION: THE POWER OF THE MIND 23
    Meditation: The Skeleton Key to the Magical 24
    Meditation: The Art of Mindfulness 25
    Meditation Techniques 26
    Why Meditate? 29
CHAPTER FOUR: YOGA: THE MAGIC OF THE PHYSICAL BODY 30
    Self-Discovery and Self Realization through Yoga 30
    A Brief History of Yoga 31
    Mystical Uses of Yoga in the Past 33
    Yoga According to Aleister Crowley 35
CHAPTER FIVE: MAGICAL ASTRAL TRAVEL TECHNIQUES 41
    What is Astral Projection? 41
    Why You Should Learn to Astral Project 42
    The Astral Body 44

THE QABALAH AND THE TREE OF LIFE 45
ASTRAL PROJECTION METHODS 46
ASTRAL PROJECTION TECHNIQUES 47

CHAPTER SIX: BUILDING YOUR SACRED SPACE 52
YOUR ALTAR 52
CREATING YOUR ALTAR 53
CARE FOR YOUR ALTAR 55
CLEANSING YOUR ALTAR'S SPACE 56
WHAT TO DO WHEN THERE'S NO ROOM 57

CHAPTER SEVEN: THE TOOLS OF THE CRAFT 59
THE MOST POWERFUL TOOL OF ALL 66

CHAPTER EIGHT: PREPARING FOR RITUAL 67
WHAT'S A RITUAL? 67
ELEMENTS AND COMPONENTS OF RITUALS 68
THE IMPORTANCE OF RITUALS 69
PREPARING FOR YOUR RITUAL 70
THE PROGRESSION OF THE RITUAL 72

CHAPTER NINE: PERFORMING PURIFICATION 74
PURIFICATION 74
BANISHING 76
STAYING CLEAN 76
CROWLEY'S LESSER BANISHING RITUAL OF THE PENTAGRAM 77
PREPARING FOR THE LESSER BANISHING RITUAL OF THE PENTAGRAM 78
THE PROCESS 79

CHAPTER TEN: THREE METHODS OF INVOCATION 81
CROWLEY'S THREE METHODS OF INVOCATION 82
ASSUMPTION OF GODFORMS 83

CHAPTER ELEVEN: THE ART OF DIVINATION 85
DIVINATION DEFINED 85
DIVINATION VS. FORTUNE TELLING 85
DIVINATION: SUBJECTIVE AND PERSONAL 86
PRACTICAL DIVINATION EXERCISES 87

CHAPTER TWELVE: MORE MAGICAL PRACTICES 92

- Consecration 92
- Evocation 93
- Magical Formulas 93
- Magical Record 94
- Magical Weapons 94
- Mineral Magic 95
- Stones and their Magical Uses 96

CONCLUSION 100
PART 2: MOON SPELLS 102
INTRODUCTION 103
SECTION 1: MOON MAGIC ESSENTIALS 105
CHAPTER 1: MOTHER MOON: HER POWER AND SYMBOLISM 106
- Greek Myths 107
- The Moon and the Triple Goddess 108
- The First Triple Goddess 110
- The Symbolism of the Moon Phases 110

CHAPTER 2: LUNAR PHASES: WHEN TO WORK MOON SPELLS 113
- Special Phases 123

CHAPTER 3: MOON SPELLCASTING: TOOLS AND PREPARATION 126
- Tools for Spell Casting 127
- Preparing for the Spells 134

SECTION 2: PRACTICAL MOON SPELLS 138
CHAPTER 4: LOVE SPELLS 139
- Tips 140
- Lunar Phase 141

CHAPTER 5: FERTILITY SPELLS 145
- Fertility Ritual 146
- Fertility Spell 147
- Full Moon Spell 148
- Safe Childbirth Spell 150

CHAPTER 6: MONEY AND CAREER SPELLS 151
- Full Moon Money Spell 152
- Spell to Get a Job 153

NEW MOON PROMOTION SPELLS 154
NEW MOON MONEY RITUAL 155
RITUAL FOR PERFORMANCE REVIEWS 155

CHAPTER 7: MANIFESTATION SPELLS 157
FULL MOON RITUAL 158
WATER RITUAL 159
WISHES MANIFESTATION RITUAL..160
CLEANSING RITUAL 161
NEW MOON RITUAL 162

CHAPTER 8: PROTECTION SPELLS 164
ENERGY CLEANSE RITUAL 164
PROTECTION FROM ENEMIES..166
DARK MOON PROTECTION SPELL...167
BLACK SALT FOR SPIRITUAL PROTECTION 169

CHAPTER 9: BANISHING SPELLS 171
FULL MOON RELEASE RITUAL..171
SPELL TO BANISH NEGATIVITY 173
FOUR THIEVES VINEGAR TO BANISH EVIL 174
SPELL TO BANISH DEPRESSION 174
REFLECTIVE BANISHING 175
SPELL TO REMOVE CURSES 176
SPELL TO BANISH DANGER..176
SPELL TO REMOVE PEOPLE FROM YOUR LIFE..177
SPELL TO BANISH ALCOHOL ADDICTION 178
SPELL TO BANISH NEGATIVE INFLUENCES 179

SECTION 3: OTHER WAYS TO WORK WITH THE MOON 181

CHAPTER 10: MOON WATER, CRYSTALS, AND OILS 182
MOON WATER 182
CRYSTALS...185
MOON OIL..188

CHAPTER 11: MOON GODDESS RITUALS 190
DRAWING DOWN THE MOON RITUAL..190
INVOKING ARTEMIS (FULL MOON RITUAL) 192

  FULL MOON RITUAL FOR DIANA 194
  WICCAN ESBAT 195
CHAPTER 12: CREATING YOUR OWN UNIQUE MOON RITUALS **197**
  UNIQUE FULL MOON RITUAL 198
  NEW MOON RITUAL 199
  TIPS FOR CREATING YOUR RITUALS 201
CONCLUSION **202**
HERE'S ANOTHER BOOK BY MARI SILVA THAT YOU MIGHT LIKE **203**
YOUR FREE GIFT (ONLY AVAILABLE FOR A LIMITED TIME) **204**
REFERENCES **205**

Part 1: Magic

Unlock the Power of Natural Forces and Learn Techniques Such as Purification, Divination, Invocation, Astral Travel, Yoga and More

Introduction

What a curious choice you've made by reading this book. You're either a longtime practitioner of magic, or you're a beginner who's looking for guidance. Either way, you are reading this for a reason. Something has drawn you to this book, out of all the many others out there. So, stick with it.

You can skip to the areas that interest you most if you've been practicing magic for a while now. If you're a complete beginner, then it would be in your best interests to begin at the beginning.

You will find this work is unlike any other out there. It is up to date, very easy to understand, and will not leave you scratching your head about what's going on with each page. The exercises and methods found here are very simple to follow. That said, do not allow their simplicity to fool you, as they are ten times as powerful as they are simple.

Read this book on magic with an open mind and put everything you're about to learn into practice. What you will discover is a world full of magic and wonder, one in which you continue to live out your True Will, moment by moment. Imagine living a life where you are productive and grow in spirit and truth, whether you're awake or asleep.

Imagine understanding that the world around you brims with even more activity than you can perceive, and there are energies you can work with to sculpt the life meant for you and no one else. These are the treasures you're about to discover.

This text is not necessarily the last bus stop with all things magical, but it will offer you the most basic, useful, practical information that, when applied, will definitely pay off in huge ways! Highlight important sections, reread chapters of the book, and go off on a wonderful adventure as you explore the ideas in these pages when you're done.

By the time you're through, you will have learned so much, and if I've done my job right, you'll conclude that you have not learned enough... Nor could you ever. The whole point of this book is to give you what you need to set a fire in your soul and set you off and running on a quest to be more than you already are. It will help you express all the wonderful gifts that remain dormant in you and find that as far as the magical life and quest for knowledge go, there is no end. There is only more depth... and that is a wonderful thing, indeed.

Chapter One: Acknowledging the Magic Within

Let us begin our exploration of magic by getting into the etymology and origin of the word "magic." We will focus on magic in the context of the great Aleister Crowley's definitions, looking at it through the lens of his Thelema. Crowley was a mystic, a writer, and a ceremonial magician, a master of the most complex and elaborate rituals in magic.

Crowley developed the esoteric philosophy of The Thelema early in the 1900s. The word *thelema* has a simple yet potent meaning to the mystic who sees beyond the ordinary. It means "will." Or, if you prefer another way to put it:

- "To want"
- "To wish"
- "To will"
- "Purpose"

Without getting too into the *thelema* and off the subject of what you're interested in, lets wrap this up by clarifying the three key pillars that hold up the thelemic philosophy according to Crowley:

1. **"Do What Thou Wilt' Shall be the Whole of the Law."** In present-day English, that means "'Do what you will' shall be the whole of the Law." It is on you as the true follower of the Thelema to seek the path that resonates with you the most and follow it. This path is your True Will. It is your resonating moment by moment with nature. It is you fulfilling the highest calling for your soul.

2. **"Love is the Law, Love Under Will."** This means you must understand that at the very core of the Thelema is love. Love reigns, but it is only secondary to discovering what your true mission is and manifesting the your authentic destiny or will.

3. **"Every Man and Every Woman is a Star."** Just as every star in the universe has its own place in space, and just as every star is unique and unmistakably itself, so also is everyone on Earth. As a follower of the Thelema, understand that everyone has their own unique fingerprint, with their very own Wills, which they must fulfill. You have a path all your own, just like the cashier at Starbucks or the business executive looking pensively at his watch. Since everyone has their unique paths, there needn't be any conflict with one another.

Now let us get back to magic. Magic, according to Aleister Crowley, is a term that creates a striking distinction between performance magic such as what you'd see on a stage — pulling out rabbits from hats, sawing people in half — and the occult. The latter is more about mysticism and mysteries that cannot be described by scientists and cannot be neatly packaged as a religious fairy tale.

Crowley defines magic as "the Science and Art of causing Change to occur in conformity with Will," which involves the run-of-the-mill willful acts, and rituals. Basically, you can create the change you seek in any object, as long as that transformation is possible and allowed by the laws of nature.

The only way for you to understand your real self is for you to act in accordance with your true will. If you're going to make this happen, then you'll never find a better path or method than the practice of magic. In other words, it is vital that you come to accept the presence of magic within you. Your true will is the meeting point between your destiny and your free will.

In the words of Master Crowley, on page 134 of Magic, Book 4, *"One must find out for oneself, and make sure beyond doubt, who one is, what one is, why one is... Being thus conscious of the proper course to pursue, the next thing is to understand the conditions necessary to following it out. After that, one must eliminate from oneself every element alien or hostile to success, and develop those parts of oneself which are especially needed to control the aforesaid conditions."*

The Goal of Magic

You may wonder where the "k" in this spelling of magic comes from. No, it's not a typo; this is how it was spelled in Early Modern English, and this is the spelling you will find in all of Aleister Crowley's writings. Again, it distinguishes childish tricks and real power through knowledge and application of the occult.

With magic, you can create the change you seek by simply using the right kind of force, in the right amount, through the right method and appropriate mechanisms. It is a science because you've got to look at yourself under a figurative microscope so you can understand what makes you uniquely you. It's also an art because you've got to be able to take what you learn and apply it to your life in a way that yields results.

You can't divorce magic from the paranormal. Rather than let this frighten you, embrace it because the paranormal effects of magic will prove themselves useful to your development. Crowley himself testifies his own experiences with these powers, which appeared when he didn't really need them. He warned that they could be incredibly seductive and throw you off the path of discovering yourself. You do have to reject these powers or "Siddhi" as they are known in Ayurvedic philosophy.

Yet, Crowley admits there is still good to be had from these effects. Whenever you feel doubtful about the reality or potency, having these experiences will remind you that it's all very real and even the most advanced student must deal with these doubtful thoughts at times. So, the best way to use them is as a reminder that you are, indeed, on your true path.

A Rational Explanation of Magic

Unfortunately, there's a lot of misinformation about magic, especially since it is codified in metaphors and symbols which easily lend themselves to misinterpretation by the uninitiated or ignorant. So, what is magic really about? Well, keep your mind open, and prepare to be blown away.

Reconsidering Crowley's definition of magic, you'd think that magic means you can use supernatural powers to turn a pig into a unicorn or give a goat five extra legs. This is not the change that Crowley means by any stretch of the imagination. That's only possible in animation.

So, what is magic in the most rational and practical of definitions? Say you're thirsty. Your will is to quench your thirst. So, you go to the fridge, get yourself something to drink, and then you're no longer thirsty. You've created the change you sought in your body, or your physical reality, using your own will.

If magic were only about simple things such as quenching your thirst or feeding yourself, there'd be no point in reading this book or to the study of magic itself. You already know how to do those basic things. The example was simply to illustrate in the most basic way what magic is about. It is simply the process of actualizing the ideas you have in your mind by using your will to make them concrete. In other words, you use your will to manifest your desires into 3D reality.

Please realize that this doesn't mean everything you do is magical. For you to perform magic, you must possess the magician's mindset. You must understand innately that all the physicality is basically clay for you to mold into whatever form you will it to assume. Again, this has nothing to do with defying the preset laws of nature or physics. If anyone tells you they can fly off a building, I encourage you to cock your head at them and squint suspiciously while backing away ever so slowly. It simply understands that your life is yours to craft into whatever you want it to be. This is the magician's mindset. This is the position of true, pure power and limitlessness.

The key to having power in your life is to know who you are, what you are, and your reason for being. Once you have this knowledge, the next step on the path is to set a goal for yourself, preferably one you deeply resonate with. You must know exactly what it is you've got to do to produce these goals. The final step is to get rid of anything within you — within your mind — that would hinder making those goals a reality while honing the skills you'd need to make it all happen for you.

Say your goal is to become a world-renowned teacher on the laws of the universe. Well, you'd most definitely need to have some medium or platform to share your teachings with the world. That could mean conferences where you speak to crowds, or it could mean having a Twitter account where you drop 160 words of wisdom per tweet for people to follow along and digest.

However, you might have a weakness that would keep you away from achieving your goals. Say you're afraid of sharing your ideas, or you're deathly scared of having to speak to crowds. What do you do to eliminate this weakness? Well, you could gradually expose yourself to situations where you must speak with five, maybe ten people at a time.

You could also take classes on public speaking while you're at it, so you gain confidence and lose your fear of addressing the masses. You could attend karaoke, sing a song or two. You could recite poetry on open mic night. Whatever you do, you do it with the awareness that you're shaping your reality into one where you've achieved your set goal of teaching the world about how the universe works.

Magic and NLP

Let's talk about summoning demons — and try to get rid of preconceived notions about what demons are or aren't, for the time being. Assume that each day, you have a ritual that involves summoning a demon that allows you to speak with confidence and charisma, with no fear, no hesitation. This demon makes you feel invincible, strong, powerful.

Now, assume you're at a Ted Talk, and you're just about to start your presentation, so you summon this demon to assist you, so you don't fear the crowd, and you don't worry about whether you will fumble. This technique is not as outlandish as you think. It's simply Neuro-Linguistic Programming, which you may have heard of as NLP.

A very popular NLP technique is to assume that you're a giant. You're tall, strong, powerful, and you tower over everyone else in the room. When you imagine you're this powerful giant, you feel it in your body and in your mind. Now, when you have that feeling in you, you could press your thumb and middle finger to each other at the tips. That action is known as an anchor, meaning you're anchoring the feeling of being that invincible giant to the simple act of touching your middle finger and thumb together. Now, whenever you do that, the feeling automatically comes over you. You can use this anchor when you are about to give a speech, or you simply need a shot of courage and power. This works with the very same mechanism that happens when you hear a song, and your body and mind are instantly transported to the time and place when you first heard it.

The whole point of this is to make it clear to you that there's nothing crazy or unnatural about magic or rituals. It all has its roots in the human psyche. So if you ever assumed that you could make a portal appear in the sky using magic or that you could quite literally lift a mountain with your mind and cast it into the sea, then you should disabuse yourself of that notion right now. That last bit about casting a mountain into the sea was a popular parable in the Bible. A parable is a metaphor, a story that symbolizes an idea or a concept. To take it literally is foolishness. As a magic practitioner, you will continue to develop a sense of symbology and find true meaning where others lose their way.

The Power is Within You

People like Aleister Crowley understand that we all have within us the power to sculpt reality as we wish. We have the innate ability to take control of our lives and make of it what we will. This is echoed in the Thelemic principle that says, "Do what thou wilt." Sadly, many people have been deceived into thinking they must bow to an external God to achieve what they desire, without realizing that they themselves are God. That's right. You are God, master of your fate. Turn to no other than yourself to achieve your dreams.

The holy books are full of stories because it was the only way to explain psychology in terms that people could relate to. The wise men and women of those times turned to story and allegory to explain the mind's power, the power that lies within us all. Unfortunately, people have taken the allegorical and assumed that they're all literal.

This explains alchemy. It was never about the actual transformation of other materials into gold. It was simply a means to explain that to become the highest, grandest version of yourself, you will need to rid yourself of everything in you and about you that would stand in the path of you becoming golden. This means working on yourself psychologically.

Psychologist Jung knew of the true meaning of esoteric and gnostic teachings and made them a core part of his life's work. When you purify yourself by getting rid of your weaknesses and all tendencies that would stop you from achieving greatness, you transform yourself from unremarkable material to pure gold.

When Crowley spoke of understanding who you are, what you are, and why you are, he was referring to psychology. The more insight you have on yourself, the more you will increase in power. Your awareness will continue to grow and expand, which will lead to you having new, different, powerful ideas in your mind, which you can then use to shape your life as you desire.

The true magician is powerful because she has no doubt about who she is, what she is, and why she exists. She doesn't even call herself a magician. The word "magician" comes with a lot of baggage. Say to someone, "I'm a magician," and they will either assume you're nuts or ask for tickets to your next show, even if they have no intention of attending it. She is more about bringing her goals to pass in physical reality, understanding that the word "magic" is problematic.

In a Nutshell...

Magic is the art and science of manifesting using ritual, imagination, archetypes, and symbols. With ritual, you harness the energy needed to create your reality, to influence things to go your way.

There are those who assume that it is a thing of madness. "It's all in your head," they tell you. It's all made up. Yet, it is hard to dismiss the effect that magical rituals have on your body. You feel the crackling energy, and you sense the changes in your way of thinking. You see actual changes in the way you live your life and actual results. For something that's all in your head, the magic of ritual is undeniably powerful. You can easily say to the nonbelievers, as Lon Milo DuQuette wrote, "It's all in your head... You just have no idea how big your head is."

Some people look at magic through the lens of energy. They believe that the practitioner of magic simply generates energy that interacts with matter so it creates change, whether near or far. Neuroscientists argue this energy is self-generated, arising from your brain and nervous system. Others, including quantum physicians, say that consciousness or energy is what the universe is made of itself; and the latter is proving more and more to be the case. Read Dr. Dean Radin's "Real Magic" for more on the subject of thought-influencing matter.

When it comes to magic, the last mindset assumes that it all happens by asking for the help of spirits or angels to make our goals come to pass. To accept this would mean we must also accept there is a whole other spectrum of life to which we're not privy as humans, a whole other universe we can interact with by deliberately being aware of it. Whether these beings do exist, simply acting on the assumption that they're real and will help you do produce remarkable results each time.

If you recall nothing else about magic, then keep these three things in mind:

- **Magic is About Intention.** You know what you *really* want, not what you only think you want. This is your intention, unconditioned and untamed by doubts or beliefs about being unworthy or not deserving of your intention. You will know your objective by how much joy it gives you and how much it effuses your whole being with light and enthusiasm.

- **Magic is About Attention.** You must focus on your purpose with an unwavering mind and heart. The more you can feel it, imagine it, and accept it, the faster you allow the intention to unfold and crystalize into 3D reality.

- **Magic is About Action.** You cannot just sit at home, visualize a bag of money in your closet, or a lover in your bed, and then just wait home for those things to come to you. There is action involved. You act as a show of faith that your goal has come to pass, and you put yourself in a position where you're ready to receive your goal. Things do work out on their own after your ritual, but you should do the things you have to do to be ready to receive the physical manifestation of your blessing.

Chapter Two: Magical Law: Do What You Will

What comes to your mind when you read the magical law, "Do what thou wilt?" The license to do whatever you please, whenever, no matter the consequences? Well, that's not what Crowley meant by that. Sadly, this phrase is often misunderstood, even by those who claim to be in the know when it comes to occult matters. "Do what you will" doesn't mean you should engage in debauchery or overindulgence. Crowley's original philosophy wasn't losing yourself to whatever whims come upon you. His quote was referring to True Will.

Discovering Your True Will: The Key to Transformation

To learn your True Will, you must find your True Self. When you learn this, then you must do just that. You must "do what you will." It's not about giving yourself carte blanche to go on a killing spree or sacrifice the young and innocent. Do what you will by discovering your life's true purpose, finding your diving path, and staying on that path, ignoring all else.

Crowley, ever-prolific, gave various definitions during his life. True Will is essentially your energy. It is that which you are to spend your lifetime or lifetimes expressing. Crowley puts it beautifully when he says, "True Will is the reason for your incarnation". According to Crowley in Magic Without Tears, to discover yours, "You must find an answer to the question: 'How did I come to be in this place at this time, engaged in this particular work?'"

The essence of "do what thou wilt" is simply this: The only right you have is to do your True Will at all times – in thought, word, and deed. To be clear, at no point will your Truth ever cause others pain or despair. It will never rob other stars like you of their own rights to follow their own truth. This principle does not give you permission to hurt others willfully, take advantage of them, or put them in a dangerous position.

Find your True Will. When you do, remember that it will not involve cheating others or being dishonest. Nor will it involve tricking people into doing things they wouldn't ordinarily do of their own free will against their best interests, manipulating them, or any of that ugliness.

Crowley likened it to the Tao. Most people assume that it is all about action, but it's about much more than that. It is energy you manifest in whatever form you will. Think about the Tao for a moment. For following the Tao, there's no conscious thought. It's all energy flowing along naturally, much like a river flows downstream, unaided and unimpeded. It all moves along with the force of authenticity. The river isn't thinking to itself, "I'm headed to the sea." The river isn't being guided by anything other than the natural position of the rocks and the riverbed around it. It moves with its authentic, natural laws as coded in nature. It moves with the Tao.

In Magic Without Tears, chapter XXXIV, Crowley likens it to a planet moving in harmony with other planets while on its own path. When another planetary body comes too close, the planet makes a little adjustment with no force, no disagreement, all so it can continue in its own orbit. This suggests what we covered in chapter one, that everyone is a star in their own right, with their own to discover and pursue. When you have found yours, it will not impinge on another's ability to follow their Truth. Every star remains in a state of balance with every other star. In being your authentic self, you will create balance in your life, and this balance will ripple out to the universe, creating the lasting change you seek in your reality.

The Inscription on the Door to the Mystical: Man, Know Thyself

You must identify yourself to access the divine mysteries of the universe and harness them for your good and the good of others. To know yourself, you must be yourself and observe who that self really is. But how can you be yourself in a world that continues to insist you shouldn't color outside the lines? How do you become authentic in a world that says from one side of its mouth, "Be unapologetically you," and on the other side it says, "Okay, reign it back in. That's too much 'you' going on." Dare to explore yourself outside of what society and media say is okay, and you're crucified for it.

It's so hard to be who you are since it means you must deal with disagreements with family, friends, and the world in general. It almost seems pointless. Why deliberately start a fight with the whole world on one side and you standing alone?

Here's why it's worth it for you to know yourself: It's the only way you will ever find pure, lasting happiness. If you do not know yourself, your real Self, then you cannot find your True Will; and if you cannot find it, let alone act on it, then you will be condemned to a life brimming with sadness and dissatisfaction. Crowley writes in Magic in Theory and Practice that each one of us is "unsatisfactory to himself until he has established himself in his right relation with the Universe." This right relation is your True Will, born of self-knowledge.

Listen, if you're doing anything outside of your this, then it is a waste of time and effort. Those who go against it, ignorantly or by choice, will find that their hopes and dreams are like a river attempting to go from moving downstream to flowing upstream: An impossibility.

You must know yourself, so you can let go of hanging branches and treacherously smooth stones, and simply allow yourself to be carried downstream to your desire, which is ever present, and just waiting for you to stop fighting it.

Going downstream doesn't mean your path will be easy or there will not be stumbling blocks along your way. You'll have to deal with these things; that's the nature of life. You'll deal with pushback in the form of family, friends, and society, who will not be able to understand your purpose. They mean well, but often, yours runs contrary to the plans they have for you, and so they will fight it. You can be sure of that. Still, the reward of staying true to your authentic self is *very much* worth it.

Do all you can to make a lion bark and a frog meow. No matter what, you will never succeed. But allow each animal their natural sound, and you have discovered the secret to moving ahead in life. You can learn that the inertia of the Universe can carry you much further along your path than you can by trying to muscle your path into make something work out that was never for you in the first place!

Dispelling the Myths Surrounding the Magical Law

Again, there are too many misconceptions surrounding the *magical law*. To help you stay the course and make progress with magic, you must know the truth. So, let's rid ourselves of these lies and misunderstandings.

Myth #1: You Only Find Your True Will at a Particular Point in Time. For some reason, there's a myth going around that there's a certain moment that you get to discover what your true will is. This myth suggests that while you may not know your will, at some point in the future, it will come upon you in an experience or a flash of insight.

The truth is as penned by Crowley in <u>Liber II: Message of the Master Therion</u>: "The will is but the dynamic aspect of the self..."

In other words, it is just you expressing yourself naturally. Your true nature will be expressed, whether in full or diluted, with preconceived notions about who you should be. So, we're always engaging in it. If we are, what then is the purpose of all this "find your True Will" talk? It's simple: The point being made is that we could do a better job of doing what we want, by being more aware of what we want and doing so with more commitment and intention. Sudden insights do happen, but that event doesn't change that your Truth is moment-by-moment, dynamic, and worth pursuing at all costs.

Myth #2: True Will Can Only be Found in the Distant Future. Much like the previous myth, people think to themselves, "I may not have a clue what my Will is right now, but I'll know it when I see it... in the future... hopefully." This is not an unreasonable thought, but again, the magician should remember that every day, every moment, we're acting on our will to some degree. Perhaps, rather than saying "'Find your True Will," we might say "Become more aware of your True Self and seek to understand it better."

When you think of it as a thing to be discovered, it makes you less eager to do or be what you are at the moment. It makes you defer things to a later date. You look around you as you live the crummy life you don't want and say, "If only I knew what my *True Will* is!" when it would be even more beneficial to consider the present circumstances and see what can be done in the now.

Myth #3: Either You're Acting on Your True Will – or You're Not. Will is not a black and white thing. There are many shades of gray. It all comes down to how much you pursue it. Remember this, and you'll find the journey much easier since you won't be bogged down by doubt or guilt about whether you're staying true to yourself. You know that you're following your path, and the only adjustment you need to make is to be more engaged and intentional about remaining faithful to your path 100 percent.

Myth #4: True Will is Only One Thing, and it Never Changes. This is far from the truth. Will has nothing to do with "the perfect job" or anything like that. It is a combination of your various talents, hobbies and proclivities, dreams, and aspirations. It will involve so much more than just wearing one hat as "teacher," or "doctor," or "mother."

You cannot isolate a single thing and say, "It is my will to be a parent." Well, if all you are is a parent, what are you when you *go to work*? Are you a parent at your legal firm? Well, obviously not; you're a lawyer. When you get back home, do you play attorney to your kids and family? These questions may seem silly, but they serve to illustrate that it isn't just tied to one thing; it's very dynamic, changing from moment to moment.

Myth #5: True Will Can be Summed Up in a Phrase. I hope you see why this one's a myth. If it is dynamic (and it is), then how do you sum it up in a neat phrase? Now, it is beneficial to try to do that, so you have an expression by which to judge whether you're following your Truth *at the moment*. Say a phrase goes, "It is my Will to have the fullness of health," which would mean you have no business eating that third pack of candy bars.

Well, then, what other phrases would you have to define your character when confronted with a situation that tempts you to cheat? And what other phrase would you have when faced in a place where you question the abundance of the universe and its availability to you? You cannot sum it up in a phrase because it is beyond words. Crowley put it this way: *"Also reason is a lie; for there is a factor infinite and unknown; all their words are skew-wise."* You can find this quote in Liber AL vel Legis, II:32.

Myth #6: Finding Your True Will Means Having a Mystical Experience. You do not need a highly evolved being to appear and tell you what it is. You need not have ayahuasca before you know. You don't need to "attain enlightenment." Sure, these experiences might lend you clarity and help keep your ego in check, but remember that Will is always present, and it's constantly acted upon to a degree, and it can be more intentionally expressed.

You don't need a special mystical background to know that a certain relationship or friendship is no longer in harmony with you. You don't need a mystical experience to let you know that time to switch career paths or time to follow your dreams actively. Do not mistakenly assume that your lack of a magical understanding gives you a free hall pass to avoid your Will.

Myth #7: Your True Will is True for Everyone Else. There is no such thing as the "ideal magician." There's no gold standard by which one can measure all Thelemites. It is not your place to decide for others what is right or wrong for them or what their True Will is. In <u>The Vision</u>, it is written, "The man of the earth is adherent. The lover giveth his life unto the work among men. The hermit goeth solitary and giveth only of his light unto men."

Put another way: Some people are of the earth, others are hermits, and a few are lovers. It is different for us all. One might seek spiritual illumination, and another may seek to live a life free of such concerns. None of these are wrong, and to insist that your path is the one true path is not only very egotistical, but it also hints of a holier-than-thou attitude, and is the complete antithesis of full liberty, which is the hallmark of the Law.

Myth #8: Your Will Has No Connection with Others Around You. While we're all individual stars, we're all interconnected in the same galaxy. We're affected by the world around us, and in turn, we affect the world as well. In other words, your actions are not contained in a bubble; they ripple out into the universe.

If it is your will to eat only meat, then animals are affected. If it is your will to eat only plants, plants are affected. If it is to be generous, well, you can be charitable only to others. To attain enlightenment, that means your environment and circumstances must be affected in some way to allow you that experience.

With this in mind, if you notice you keep facing a lot of difficulties when you do certain things, you might want to think of it as a message saying you need to change what you're doing or how you're doing it, rather than being so stubborn and insisting "My way or the highway."

Myth #9: True Will Exempts You From Suffering. Again, finding and following it to the best of your abilities does not mean you will not face adversity. Suffering is a part of life. We fall ill; we lose people, we forget stuff, we die. That's just life. Just because you're experiencing something doesn't mean you're automatically a failure at staying true to your will. Suffering allows you to grow, learn, and become more than you ever were.

As a true Thelemite, you're not interested in transcending the physical material world. You're not looking to avoid pain and suffering. Acknowledging suffering as part of life sets you free from the bondage of unnecessary feelings. There lies the distinction. A lot of misery is not the natural kind, nor is it needed. Instead, it is born of the undisciplined mind, fed by lies and misconceptions both from within and without. It is this *unnecessary* suffering that it exempts you from.

Myth #10: True Will Exempts You From Conflict. Like suffering, differences cannot be avoided in life. There will always be those who do not see things how you do. Even as you do this practice (and they do theirs), they will not always see eye-to-eye with you. There's nothing inherently wrong with a disagreement. The trouble is in how the difference is *perceived*.

When doing this and allowing others the right to follow theirs, you come to understand that it's okay to perceive things differently. You let go of the impulse to insist that your approach is the right way or the only way —a mindset that causes a lot of disagreements to devolve into terrible outcomes like betrayal, war, and oppression.

It doesn't mean conflicts end. You just come to an understanding you have no right to place your standards and expectations on anyone else, just as they have no right to impinge on your chosen manner of self-expression or beliefs. This is why it says in AL III:42, "...argue not, convert not, talk not overmuch!"

With these myths debunked, it should be even clearer in your mind right now and should help you grow in awareness in every moment.

Chapter Three: Meditation: The Power of the Mind

That you're reading this right now says that you know just how vital it is for you to find your True Will. It says you're willing to explore it, to pursue it, and allow yourself to express it more each day. For that, commend yourself.

True Will does not readily make itself obvious, particularly to those who haven't spent time looking for it. If only it were as simple as figuring out your career, then you could at least have somewhere to start your search! You now know that True Will is about so much more than that. It is your very reason for being, for breathing.

As an initiate of magic, it is your duty to not only discover your True Will but to act it out to the best of your abilities, from one moment to the next. This is the purpose of real magic. Everything else is simply fluff and feathers. It seems so simple, and it is, theoretically. With actual practice, it can be rather difficult.

You already know that how to realize all you want in life is to follow your bliss, allow your heart or joy to guide you to what matters the most to you. But such sentiments never make it clear that these things are not simply a given. Becoming the grandest and best version of yourself doesn't simply happen. It's never been that way. It never will be. There is an element of work.

To assume these desirable traits just fall into one's lap is the same as assuming that all you need to do to build muscles is to just sit and do nothing. You've got to train. You've got to break down muscle to allow it to repair itself so that you become stronger and develop even more muscle and strength. You'll also need guidance so that you do not train in a way that makes your efforts futile, at best – or puts you in danger, at worst.

The same principle of working out your body to build muscles applies to discovering your True Will and exercising it. You will need to train and pay attention to who you're now being, so you can adjust accordingly until you align with the person you'd like to become, which is the greatness you know you are. To achieve this greatness, you will need practice. You'll need tools and you'll need various techniques and methods to train yourself. The methods and tools you need the most are meditation and magic. It is to the former we will give our attention in this chapter.

Meditation: The Skeleton Key to the Magical

There is no method to help you connect with the magical within you that works better than meditation. This is as old as time itself. It is very precise, and it always yields results without fail if you use methods that are authentic and not the run-of-the-mill garbage peddled by charlatans who would have you believe that they have the key to your salvation.

Meditation works... when you work it. You will need to remember the two stages of work as you begin your journey.

- The journey within yourself to discover your True Will.

- The application of your body, mind, and soul towards the manifestation of your True Will.

Do not let that it is work scare you away from doing what you must. It is the only work that will reward you exceedingly, far above and beyond anything else you might think of.

No one is born knowing precisely what path their life should take. If that were the case, then we'd have no struggle. We'd simply be off and running, going about the business of fulfilling our destiny. That is NOT how this works.

When you're born, you're born tabula rasa — other than your innate True Will, that is. Over time, you find you get a lot of impressions about what you should and shouldn't do, or be, or have. However, your True Will remains within you, waiting to be discovered or to be expressed even more than you allow it to be. It waits for you to become mindful of your very own divine authority over your life. You become more aware of your authority through the constant practice of meditation.

With meditation, you find that the veil that covers all eyes and makes all believe that they are simply bound to experience life happening to them falls off. You become more aware of the power within you. You learn just how powerful you are. It hits you that you have a magic wand within you — free will — which you can use to craft the life you prefer.

Meditation: The Art of Mindfulness

A very critical part of Buddhist practice is *sati*, which is awareness, or mindfulness. Mindfulness involves becoming very much conscious of the here and now. Most people's minds are either stuck in the past in regret or reminiscence or stuck in the future in worry or anticipation. Sadly, it is a rare person who is fully present in the here and now. The practice of meditation teaches you to become more aware, more present, here and now. In being tethered and grounded in the present, you're better able to decipher what your True Will dictates to you at the moment.

There are several meanings of the Buddhist word *sati*, besides mindfulness. Sati is derived from the Pali word sati and the Sanskrit smrti. Originally, smrti meant "to recollect" or "to remember" or "to bear in mind." These meanings were in connection to the Vedic tradition of memorizing sacred scripture.

According to the Satipatthana Sutta, sati means "to maintain one's awareness of reality." It further defines mindfulness (sati) as being aware that what you perceive with your senses is nothing more than illusions. This awareness allows you to see the true nature of life around you. Inevitably, the more you practice meditation, the more mindful you become, and the clearer your True Will becomes in your mind.

Meditation Techniques

Technique #1: Altered Consciousness. Find a comfortable place to sit in loose, comfy clothes, and shut your eyes. You may light incense or a candle or play some relaxing, calming music before you begin, but none of that is necessary. Such things may be a hindrance because, ideally, you want to hit a point where you can practice wherever you are, whether there are candles, music, incense, or not. These things only help you initially.

Now notice the top of your head. As you do, start to scan your body by directing that awareness from your head, slowly working your way down to your feet. As you become aware of each part of your body, allow it to relax. Notice the parts where you feel the most stress or resistance. When you feel areas on your body with tension, imagine that relaxing waves of warm light flow from the top of your head, and through these parts, clearing out all tension and unease. Do your best to relax.

Breathe in, deep as you can, making sure your lungs are filled all the way. Through your slightly parted lips, let the air go. You want each inhales and exhale to feel even deeper than the last one. Imagine your breath is like a gentle wind that blows back and forth, a never-ending, relaxing cycle. All troublesome thoughts are only clouds, which the gentle winds of your breath blow away into nothingness. Your job is not to control your thoughts. Simply allow them to pass, blown away by the wind.

Move your attention to your heart and feel the energy as it beats and moves blood around your body. Feel the love within, your love for all the people you hold dear. Feel the light in your heart. There's no need to actually see anything. Know it's there and accept it. Finally, feel the divine spark within your soul. Know that in your soul is a flame, whose light continues to burn bright and guide you along your way.

This exercise puts you in touch with the four elements of magic: By putting your body at ease, you've worked with the earth element. By sweeping away all throughs from your mind and focusing on your breath, you've worked with the air element. Focusing on your heart, love, and blood is the water element, and your soul connects you with the fire element.

Slowly countdown from ten to one as you breathe, imagining that you're writing each number on a board and then erasing it. This way, your conscious mind is ready to handle whatever task you give it. When you get to one, begin the countdown again, this time with just your inner voice, so your intuition becomes active. When you're done, you will be in an altered state. Enjoy it. This is the state of meditation, from which you can work your magic for the good of all. When you're ready to come back out of it, simply count up from one to ten, then breathe regularly, and really feel your body. Have a good stretch. If you feel out of touch, place your hands on the floor and push them in, or you can lie on your back on the floor and feel connected to it.

Technique #2: Standing Meditation. You'll want to make sure you're barefoot for this. Find somewhere quiet, shut your eyes, and keep your shoulders relaxed. Move your awareness to your feet. Feel what your feet on the floor. Pay attention to what you notice about how you're feeling. Is the middle of your feet making less contact with the ground than your heels and toes? Is the pressure even or different in spots? What about the temperature? Do you feel very little, if anything? Then try moving your feet around or rocking back and forth on them so you can feel various sensations. Notice as many of them as you can.

Technique #3: Listening Meditation. Find a place where you can hear all sorts of sounds; a restaurant, the park, a lake, or wherever. You can also do this technique while you wait at the airport or while you wait in a queue. There's no need to keep your eyes shut, though it could be incredibly helpful for some people to do that.

Now, pay attention to every sound around you. Do your best to tell them apart and notice how they contrast with one another. There are sounds that are louder, others softer. They may be deeper, and others may be shrill. Some are close, while others further off. Some are nice, while others are irritating. Notice them all. Then focus on one sound for some time before moving your attention to the next.

Technique #4: Walking Meditation. You'll want to keep your shoes and socks off for this one, too. You also want to keep your eyes open, so you don't walk into something. Whether you're with others or alone, you can do this meditation, as long as you're not disturbed. You can do this in your room, simply walking back and forth, taking your time with each step (but not as slow as, say, the sloths from that cartoon). As you move, notice your feet as they hit the ground and rise again. You can also notice all the sensations you feel in your legs, thighs, knees, calves, and angles. Just follow all the sensations you can.

Technique #5: Looking Meditation. Ideally, do this outside. If you can't get outside, then a large enough room can work just fine. You want to look at something that's close to you, perhaps a flower or your coffee mug. Look closely at every detail you find, from the varying shades to the patterns, colors, and shapes of whatever has your attention. Spend a minute or two looking at this object, then move to an object further off in the distance. Look at it with the same degree of attention for a minute or two. When you're finished, return your attention to the first object you studied, and see if you spot things you hadn't seen the first time.

Why Meditate?

As you practice these exercises, you will notice that you're much better at clearing your mind and silencing your thoughts to cut right through to the truth of any matter at the moment. You'll be more cognizant of where your thoughts are most of the time, and as such, you will be able to halt any thoughts that do not resonate with your True Will before they have the chance to gain enough traction to make a mess of things.

Meditation does a lot more than help you become aware of the moment. It helps you train your mind so it only ever does your bidding. It cannot be run on your behalf by any subliminal messages in the media or any dark, depressing stuff from the dreary world around you.

With meditation, you can tell whether you're feeding your soul with faith and the good things of life or whether you're stuffing it full of fear. You need to make sure your mind is focused on the right things. The mind does not discriminate, and it will bring you exactly what you focus on. With meditation, you're more aware of where you put your attention. Your attention is gold. Don't squander it. The best way to be sure you're not wasting it all is to make meditation a daily practice.

Chapter Four: Yoga: The Magic of the Physical Body

There are two very critical elements in terms of spiritual attainment, according to the law of Thelema. One is magic. The other is Yoga.

Self-Discovery and Self Realization through Yoga

Yoga, by its very nature, is all a process through which you discover yourself. It's not a religion, as people erroneously believe, and there's no evil in it either. It's all a practice through which you learn about who you really are and what you bring to the cosmic table, so to speak. As you go through the process of Yoga, you clear your mind of all cobwebs so you can see yourself, others, and the world around you in their truest forms.

You cannot be separate from your identity. So discovering yourself and realizing who you are is not something as basic as taking off an outfit and putting on another. Changing your character is also different from simply cramming all the verses and dogma of a religion or whatever into your mind, as most religions are guilty of doing.

Yoga is a very personal journey in which you must come to know yourself intimately. You discover your genuine nature by having your own experiences and perceiving things from your own perspective. So, think of Yoga as a science rather than a religion you can sign up for today only to renounce tomorrow. There's an entire process to it. The truly self-realized are those who have undergone the process of Yoga, which is the revelation of everything in its true form.

Here lies the key distinction between Yoga and religion: You may join a religion and not necessarily practice it to be considered part of that church, but with Yoga, you join nothing; you practice.

Many people erroneously assume that Yoga is akin to a religious sect, or a cult, or a team you join so you have the satisfaction of being a part of something bigger than you. Yoga is a set of values, tools, and virtues – all of which make up a process that leads you to become your best self physically, spiritually, and mentally. This is where many people give up on Yoga because they cannot "join" it; they can only practice it, and practice requires discipline.

Yoga is not about blind belief, but growing in wisdom and love for others. It's a solitary process, and so you must find your strength within you, and not from outside you in the form of a group. You can't join Yoga, which means *you can't quit it either.* It is your duty to yourself to continue to discover that part of you that is greater than the costume of flesh and blood you've got on right now.

A Brief History of Yoga

Yoga's history is so full of uncertainty because its sacred texts were passed on from one generation to the next by oral tradition. Plus, the instructions were mostly secretive. The earliest records of Yoga teachings were etched on palm leaves, too fragile and easy to destroy, get damaged, or be lost. While Yoga is said to have advanced over the course of 5,000 years, there are those who believe it's twice as old as that.

Four distinct periods matter the most when it comes to development, practice, and innovations in Yoga.

Pre-Classical Yoga: Yoga was initially developed over 5,000 years ago in Northern India by a civilization known as the Indus-Sarasvati. The word Yoga itself was first written in the Rig Veda, one of the oldest and most sacred texts made up of mantras, songs, and rituals used by Vedic priests called Brahmans.

The Brahmans helped to develop Yoga, slowly, along with mystic seers called Rishis. They all took time to document their beliefs, and their practices in what is called the *Upanishads* – which has over 200 scriptures, including the renowned Bhagavad-Gita, penned sometime around 500 B.C.E. What the Upanishads did was to reframe the ritual sacrifice covered in the Vedas and make it an internal process, one which involves sacrificing the ego on the altar of wisdom (jnana yoga), self-knowledge, and action (karma yoga).

Classical Yoga: Where the pre-classical stage was full of contradictory yogic ideas, the classical period had a more systematic and organized approach to the principals, because of Patanjali's Yoga-Sutras, which were written during the second century. This text goes over the ideal path of Raja Yoga, which is usually called "classical yoga." Patanjali brought order to Yoga by creating its eight-limbed path, which detailed the necessary steps and stages of the process required to gain enlightenment or Samadhi. Until now, Patanjali's Yoga-Sutras continue to influence several styles of Yoga as we know it today.

Post-Classical Yoga: Centuries after the reform Patanjali brought about, a collection of Yogis came together to form a system or series of practices that give long life and revive the body. As one, they spurned all ancient Vedic teachings and focused on using the physical body to achieve Samadhi. These Yogis created Tantra Yoga, which had techniques designed to clean both mind and body to shed off everything that tethered us to the physical world. This is how Hatha Yoga came to be.

Modern Yoga: From the late 1800s to early 1900s, there was an exodus of Yoga masters from the East to the West. These masters attracted a following, notably from the Parliament of Religions in 1893, in Chicago, when a particular Master – Swami Vivekananda – blew away his attendees with his amazing insights on Yoga. By the 1920s and 1930s, India was heavily into Hatha Yoga, thanks to

Swami Sivananda, T. Krishnamacharya, and other well-known Hatha Yoga practitioners. The first Hatha Yoga school was founded in 1924 by Krishnamacharya. Then there was the Divine Life Society, right on the Ganges River banks, established by Sivananda in 1936.

Three students — T.K.V. Desikachar, B.K.S. Iyengar and Pattabhi Jois — having been tutored by Krishnamacharya, made sure his legacy continued and that Hatha Yoga became more popular than ever. Sivananda had penned over 200 books about Yoga, set up nine ashrams, and an impressive number of yoga centers globally.

Yoga made its way to the West in little bits, until 1947, when Indra Devi set up her Hollywood Yoga studio. Ever since that happened, there have been a lot more Indian and Western Yoga teachers sharing their knowledge of Hatha Yoga and garnering followers in the millions. Now, there are all sorts of Hatha Yoga styles, which focus on various aspects of this sacred practice.

Mystical Uses of Yoga in the Past

Shamanic practices and Sadhana Yoga come together to create the magic of mystical yoga, in which your inner mystic is brought to light. The whole point of this style is to reveal your true essence, the whole point of your existence, or if you prefer, your True Will.

There are three very distinct levels which the mystical Yoga practitioner needed to remember back then. These levels remain relevant even in today's times. First, you must know the foundation of it all. This foundation comprises a routine of vital postures connected with sequences and transitional breath. Next, you must know the modification level. In other words, the practitioner would have to learn to modify the original sequences and postures to match her ability and understanding. The final level involves integration. Mystical Yoga has always been based on the mystic's personal experience as they journey to the very essence of themselves. With the integration, the mystic can better personalize the routines they've learned, giving more meaning to each.

There are so many routines involved in Mystical Yoga, from Shamanic Yoga, Hatha Flow Yoga, Restorative Yoga, and Gentle Yoga, to Mystical Vinyasa Yoga. No matter the routine, Mystical Yoga has always been a spiritual practice that follows this sequence, typically:

1. The names of deities and/or spirits and connecting energies are chanted to allow the mystic Yogi or Yogini to connect with their higher self.

2. Intentions are set once the Yogi becomes aware of his inner being so the practice deepens, and it operates on all levels, obvious and subtle.

3. Breathing exercises are done to create a deeper meditative state.

4. The practitioner warms up with easy, gentle stretches, performed while kneeling, seated, and standing. They also perform sun salutations.

5. Standing and sitting sequences are initiated.

6. The practitioner performs a series of postures in a closing sequence that works on each chakra in the body.

7. Then the practitioner goes into relaxation, using progressive relaxation of each muscle group and autosuggestion to release all blocked energy in the body, bringing the mind into a clear state with no thought, just a simple awareness of the nothingness of the universe.

8. The Yogini connects with her intention by meditating about spiritual concepts.

9. Finally, the practitioner chants the deity or spirit's name from before in appreciation, certain that her intention has been fulfilled.

Yoga According to Aleister Crowley

Crowley has written two books on Yoga and the appropriate breathing techniques. His Magic: Liber ABA (Book IV) and Eight Lectures on Yoga give the Magus (a practitioner of Magic) a lot of detail to learn meditation and Yogic breathing.

First Practice

For your first practice, Crowley suggests that you focus on breathing and nothing else. Tell yourself repeatedly, "The breath flows in," as you inhale, and as you exhale, say to yourself, "The breath flows out."

As you do this, you want to ensure you track your results. How long did you practice? You want to make sure you practiced for at least 20 minutes. Note how you did with concentration. Note how often you broke focus and notice what kind of distractions took you away from your breath. Notice your emotional, physical, and mental states as you focused on your breath. Write down the date and time and how you felt or perceived yourself and the world around you after you were done.

Crowley says that when you do this diligently, you may very well experience Samadhi or enlightenment, which is the final limb of Patanjali's Yoga-Sutras' eight limbs.

Second Practice

Here's a second practice, as explained in Liber RV, involving pranayama. Pranayama comprises the Sanskrit words prana, meaning "life," and *ayama,* which means "extend" or "draw out." Pranayama is about controlling your breath, which clears out your subtle energy channels (*nadis*) all over your body, and awakens the Kundalini (or *serpent power*) that sits at the bottom of your spine.

The kind of breathing you'll do in this practice is known as *Nadi Suddhi pranayama,* r *Anuloma pranayama,* or *Nadi Shodhana pranayama,* or in English, alternate nostril breathing.

Steps for Alternate Nostril Breathing

1. Take a seat in an asana. With your left thumb, close your right nostril. Breath out as slow as you can through your left nostril, for up to 20 seconds. Then breathe in through that same nostril for 10 seconds.

2. Next, switch thumbs, and close your left nostril this time. Breathe in through your right nostril for up to 20 seconds, and then for 10 seconds.

3. Continue to alternate your hands and do this for an hour. If you're only starting, begin with 20 minutes, and work your way up with each new session.

4. Eventually, you should exhale for 30 seconds and inhale for 15 seconds.

5. When it's easy for you to breathe for the times mentioned in the previous step (and not a moment before, warns Crowley), exhale for 15 seconds, inhale for 15 seconds, and then hold your breath for 15 seconds. Continue with this until you can do this easily for an hour.

6. Now, increase your exhale time to 40 seconds and your inhale time to 20 seconds.

7. Once this time is easy for you; exhale for 20 seconds, inhale for 10 seconds, and hold your breath for 30 seconds.

8. Doing step 7 comfortably means you're ready for harder techniques. Crowley writes that you should become proficient at a cycle with a ratio of 10:20:40 seconds, or 16:32:64, and longer. It is vital that you build up to those lengths gradually.

Crowley warns that if there's food in your stomach, it will make your practice harder, no matter how little there is. So, you want to be mindful of eating before your pranayama practice.

He adds that you must not strain yourself because you do not want to go so out of breath you breathe too fast or you gasp for air. It is important you keep your breathing full, deep, and regular. You'll need a journal to note down all the magical things you experience as you practice, as well as to analyze your results.

When you perform pranayama the right way, your body will be covered in perspiration, much different from the kind you get from heat or a workout. You can rub this sweat back into your body to gain strength. Your body will also go rigid, automatically. You will then have spasmodic movements of your body, which you're aware of even in your unconsciousness. It can seem like there's no weight to you, and an unseen force moves you. Also, your body will levitate and remain suspended for anywhere from one second to over an hour.

Third Practice

Consider this to be a walking variation of the previous pranayama practice. It's known as Bhraman pranayama or "walking breath."

Steps for Walking Breath

1. As you walk, breathe in and out, deeply and fully.

2. Chant a mantra in a rhythm that matches each footstep. You could chant *Om; Om mani padme hum; or Om Shanti, Shanti, Shanti.*

3. You'll begin the pranayama but using both nostrils and without holding your breath. Rather than breathing for specific counts, you'll breathe in tandem with your steps. You could breathe in for four steps and then breathe out for four.

4. Up the number of steps per inhale and exhale to 6 each, then 8 each, then 12, then 16, and then 24 or more if you can.

5. Next, switch it up by inhaling for 6 steps and exhaling for 12. Then you can go from 6:12 to 8:16, and move on to 12:24 or even more if you can.

6. Finally, add in the Kumbhakam, which is holding your breath. Start by inhaling for 4 steps, holding for 4 steps, then exhaling for 4 steps. Then you can move on to 2 steps per inhale, 8 steps per hold, 4 steps per exhale, and 8 steps per hold. You can up the count in a ratio of 1:4:2.

7.

Fourth Practice

1. Begin the walking pranayama from the third practice. Find your rhythm with your steps, breathing, and mantra.

2. Go faster and faster with your steps and your mantra until your walking becomes a dance.

Crowley advocates using the basic waltz rhythm for your steps (left-right-left, right-left-right, and so on). Your mantra must be in three-time. If it is dedicated to a deity, you could turn this meditation into a form of worship. However, Crowley says it's better to use a mantra that paints an abstract idea of the supreme God.

Fifth Practice

1. Begin with your walking pranayama and get into a nice rhythm with your mantra, steps, and breathing. Allow it all to become a dance.

2. Now, allow the dance to be free of your will. You do this by zoning out into a state of trance, allowing your spirit to flow through your dancing body. This is not a conscious thing. You will know when you've achieved this state. You may occasionally exercise your will, but with practice, learn to let it go.

The same phenomena as described for the second practice of alternate nostril breathing may happen again with this.

Sixth Practice

This practice involves breathing fast and shallow. It can also include meditation on your Vishuddha chakra while you chant its mantra "ham." This chakra is your throat chakra, which oversees self-expression and communication. It acts as a purifier. Through this chakra, amrita or "the elixir of life" flows down. This elixir can either be poisonous, or it can lead to immortality. With this open, you allow yourself to receive wisdom in abundance. When it's closed, decay and death follow.

1. Breathe. Make it as rapidly and shallowly as you can.

2. Get into a position you'd be in if you'd just exhaled with force. Drop your chin slightly, tucking it close to your chest while pushing your tongue against your palate.

3. You must breathe using only your throat muscles.

4. If you wish, you can increase the period between each breath.

5. As you do this, keep your attention on your Vishuddha chakra.

Seventh Practice

This one is to the point. You must breathe as rapidly and deeply as you can. It's almost the same thing as the Ujjayi breathing technique, or "the ocean breath," often used in Taoist and Hindu Yoga practices. You inhale as deeply as you can, making sure your lower belly is full, then your rib cage rises, and your upper chest and throat. It's hard to pull this off *too fast*.

This practice is almost like the Breath of Fire, a technique by Yogi Bhajan, a teacher of Kundalini Yoga. You need to breathe as fast as you can, pumping our breath using the power of your belly, in and out. When your lungs fill with air, force it all out right away.

The moment your lungs are empty, force the air back in. Soon, the rhythm will become an automatic thing. Use enough force, but don't contract your diaphragm.

Mens Sana in Corpore Sano

Mens sana in corpore sano is a Latin phrase that simply means "a healthy mind in a healthy body." As a practitioner of magic, you must guard your health zealously. This is because your body and mind are tools you use to discover and express your Will.

You are not your body, and you are not your mind either. However, your state of consciousness is often what determines your physical condition. In other words, you must be aware of what thoughts go about in your mind because those images affect your body's health. The Magus must always guard his energy, making sure to meditate and to continually seek ways to stay in touch with the divine. As you practice Yoga and meditation daily, you keep your mind and body in an optimum state that allows you to fulfill your highest goal: Your True Will.

Chapter Five: Magical Astral Travel Techniques

There is so much more to the world than what you can presently perceive. To suggest that all there is to life is the physical is not just denial, but pure foolishness and the practicing Magician knows of this. The most unbelieving skeptic would soon find her opinion changed if she had an out-of-body experience, which I mean in a very literal sense. This practice is also known as *astral projection*.

What is Astral Projection?

Astral projection, also perceived as astral travel, is the act of deliberately leaving your body or moving your consciousness away from the physical onto other realms. This begs the question, what, exactly, is leaving the body? And you might also wonder, where does this thing leave the body for?

You are not your mind, and you are not your body. You are pure consciousness or soul. When you travel the astral plane, what you're doing is turning your consciousness away from the physical plane of existence to the astral one. You may think of your consciousness as your astral body, which takes on the construct of your physical body, or any other form you will find it to take on in the astral plane.

Resist the temptation to think this is all just hogwash. Thanks to the work of scientists and curious minds as Robert Muldoon, there is now more known about the subject of astral travel. It is not mere fiction. It is real, indeed.

Astral projection is an ancient practice, and it cuts across so many cultures. We have the Theosophists of the 19th century to thank for the term "astral projection." This phenomenon often happens with constant meditation and with lucid dreaming. There are those who have managed to achieve astral travel by practicing self-hypnosis or using hallucinogenic substances. There are scientists who classify astral projection as nothing more than pseudoscience, but it is simply their willful ignorance and arrogance that keeps them from exploring a very real, very rich world that exists. Perhaps it troubles them to perceive there are things that cannot be measured using their physical tools.

Why You Should Learn to Astral Project

To properly practice magic, you must be well aware of who you are. This means you must go beyond knowing the physical person that sits right now, reading this book. You must know every aspect of yourself, for only then can you truly be in control of your life. With astral projection, it is easier and easier for you to craft a life in alignment with your True Will.

Astral projection is an excellent tool for encouraging your spiritual growth and the expansion of your awareness or consciousness. It allows you to work on your True Will from a higher plane (or the cause's plane), which affects the physical plane. With astral projection, you will learn the secrets of the universe and the keys to allow you to live an actualized life. It grants you inner vision, peeling back the veil so you can see the worlds beyond this one and gain knowledge that will rapidly advance you in all aspects of life.

While far too many people who think astral projection is a sham, it would be of immense benefit to them to experience it even once. If there's one thing most astral projectors will tell you, it is that they've lost their fear of death. They understand that all that exists is consciousness, so the physical body's death a decay don't mean the conclusion of all life. To look at it logically, if life could "end" or be "taken away," then is it truly *life*? Astral projection allows you to shed all misguided ideas about the human race's fragility and embrace your immortality.

Another argument for making the practice of astral projection a constant in your life is that it is immensely helpful for learning about your past lives, which can give incredible insight into your True Will in your present incarnation. In astral travel, you have access to the Akashic records, which allow you to see the past, the present, and even possible futures as clearly as you see the words on this page.

The Magus knows that astral projection is very important for working on inner planes. This is particularly for serving those in dire need of healing, helping those who are passing on to find peace in the "afterlife," and being a beacon of unity and love for everyone else on higher levels, and so on.

If you hope to reach out to otherworldly beings, be they people who have passed on, angels, spirits, other entities, then you can easily do so through astral travel. You can also visit any spot you want to on Earth and even worlds beyond. You can see friends and even go to places some military won't let you visit... the applications of astral projection are endless.

As you study magic, understand that it is your duty to discover the aspects of you that you haven't yet discovered. You must make conscious that which lies unconscious within you. The summary of the matter is this: To become better than who you are, accept that you are greater than you assume you are. You are beyond physical.

You are consciousness. And consciousness is everything, too vast to be contained by a label, a name, or a body.

The Astral Body

You would not be far off to think of the astral body as a vehicle through which you travel around the astral plane. The Magus with clairvoyant sight can perceive it as an aura rich with colors and make of matter of a considerably sharper and finer density than the physical body. The astral body allows desires, emotions, passions, and feelings to be expressed and transmitted between your body and your mind — the latter being of a considerably sharper vehicle than your body.

Everyone has an astral body, but too few people are aware it exists, and fewer still can keep it fully under their control with the fullness of their awareness. You then become the Magus able to keep the astral body in your control, developing it and using it, so you may reap the benefits of the many powers conferred on you.

Everyone projects astrally, whether they remember it or not. The master astral projector has learned to move her astral body at will to wherever she wants it to go. However, others often find themselves in a vague, barely remembered dream because of how primitive and underdeveloped their astral bodies are. They awaken from sleep, clueless about where they have been, what they've done, and who they've met.

When you have developed your astral body through the constant practice of astral travel, while you sleep, you are engaged in meaningful and interesting activities. You do not lose time to slumber because you are still very productive as you move about the astral plane in your astral body. Your days are no longer dull and uninteresting, and your nights are not lost to oblivion. You become the ideal, actualized magician living in a continuous, unbroken cycle of consciousness.

The astral body can travel great distances in just a moment. You could say it moves at the speed of thought. You could be on the other end of the Earth, or the Universe, in a flash.

All emotions and feelings are within your astral body. You must learn to interpret what makes up this body, as this is the key to unlocking your psyche's aspects that have remained hidden from you till this point. There is no better way to understand this aspect of yourself than to practice astral projection and hone your skills so that you're not only able to travel and explore but to remember every experience when you wake up and take up consciousness in the physical realm.

The Qabalah and the Tree of Life

The Tree of Life is a very useful tool that helps to organize a set of mystical concepts.

It is made of 10 spheres, also known as emanations or sephiroth (singular, sephira). These are all connected to one another by 22 paths. Planets are used to symbolize the sephiroth, while the paths are represented by the Hebrew alphabet and divided into the four classical elements, the twelve Zodiac signs, and the seven classical planets. In Western magic, the Tree is used as a filing system, with each path and sephira being assigned an idea, whether that form is a Tarot card, an element, a sign, or a god, among other things.

As for Crowley, it is essential for the magus to understand the Tree of Life. As he writes in Magic Without Tears: *"The Tree of Life has got to be learned by heart; you must know it backward, forwards, sideways, and upside down; it must become the automatic background of all your thinking. You must keep on hanging everything that comes your way upon its proper bough."*

Just like Yoga, the need to learn about the Tree of Life isn't just about magic. It's about being able to know, inside and out, your spiritual blueprint. You can use the Tree to figure out where you want to travel astrally, decide which god you want to invoke, and so on.

Astral Projection Methods

There are several methods for you to will your astral body out and into the astral plane. Some people accomplish this through lucid dreams, where they learn they are dreaming and then project themselves out of their dreams and into the astral plane. Others use drugs to achieve astral projection — though I must warn that you would do well to stay away from this route. It is important for you to be completely in charge of your faculties and not under the influence of substances that can take away from your experience or lead you down undesired paths.

With that said, we'll have a look at the methods you can use to begin astral projection the right way, but first, we'll get into the preparations you need to make to learn astral travel.

Dream Recollection

For you to be a successful astral projector, you need to improve your dream recollection. For most people, when they wake up in the morning, they are quick to forget most details about their dreams, if not all of them. Maybe you can relate to this.

To increase your dream recollection, the first thing you should do is intend to recall your dreams each night when you go to bed. If you often wake up to use the bathroom during the night, you can set this intention to summon your dreams each time. You could either tell yourself mentally or out loud, "I will remember all my dreams tonight," then go to bed knowing you will. Do this night after night, and your memory will improve.

Another thing you absolutely must do is get a journal for your dreams. The very act of writing your dreams down does two essential things: First, it tells your subconscious mind that remembering your dreams is meaningful to you now, and so it should do all it can to help you retain those memories. Next, it helps you see a pattern emerge in your dreams so that the next time you're dreaming, you're more likely to become aware that it's all a dream when "illogical" things happen ... like a man on a cotton candy cloud in the sky saying the temperature is a nice, green unicorn.

Typically, when you dream, nonsensical things like the previous example don't make much of a blip in your mind. In real life you might stop to ask, "What's going on? Why is there a man in the sky? How is he riding a cloud? How come the cloud is cotton candy? What kind of temperature is a 'nice, green unicorn?" In your dream, you wouldn't bother because your critical thinking abilities have gone to sleep on you.

So, as you note your dreams in your journal, you will become aware of the irrationality of it all, and the next time you have something odd happen in a dream, you're more likely to become lucid. The more you become lucid, the more in charge you will be of your mental processes. The more lucid you become, the more you'll be able to remember, and the better your dream recall, the higher your chances of achieving astral travel.

Astral Projection Techniques

Technique #1: Consciousness Transfer. Make sure you're in your quiet space, alone, so no one can bug you. Dress comfortably and make sure the room is at a temperature where you won't feel too warm or too cold. Now, sit or lie in a comfortable position in which you can remain relaxed for an hour. Adjust as needed right away, so you don't make adjustments that jolt you out of your altered state later.

Now, shut your eyes and breathe in deep and slow, allowing all physical tension, negative emotions, thoughts, and intentions to melt away from you with each breath. If this is your first time, you may need about ten or twenty minutes to do a body scan. Start from the top of your head to the soles of your feet, progressively relaxing each body part and imagining a warm, soothing wave of relaxation undoing all tense knots in your body. Do not rush this process.

When you feel well relaxed and at peace, you may now count down from ten to one or chant a mantra for as long as you need until you get into a state of altered consciousness. Don't worry about needing the state to be deep. You'll find over time that *lighter is better*.

Now it is time to build your astral body or your light body. Know the form you want it to assume. You can keep it simple and let it adopt the same form as your physical body. Imagine this body coming together bit by bit, just a few feet away from where your physical body rests.

Next, you must project into this light body your mental energy and energy you draw either from the sky or from the earth. This way, your energy isn't depleted, and you can use the energy abundant in nature to create what you desire. All you must do is mentally connect with the earth or the sky and then see that stream of energy moving from either of those into the light body you're charging. Forget about obstructions like the ceiling or walls or the floor, as those cannot stand in the way of divine energy. If you can't stop being distracted by them, you can create a hole in the ceiling or wall or floor in your mind's eye and see the energy move through it. In time, you will realize this is unnecessary. Do not be shocked to find that the concept of time has lost all meaning. Allow the process to take place with no worries about time.

When your light body has become stable and solid to you, mentally assign its duty to it. You are responsible for this body, and you must dismantle this body when it has achieved its purpose so it doesn't follow you around till it's drained or cause issues for other astral travelers.

Tell the light body what you want it to do. Do not use flowery language. Be as direct and literal as you can be, and back up the words of power with images in your mind for what you expect it to achieve. After doing this, it's time to move your consciousness to the light body. Shift your awareness from your physical body to your light body. Do not do this by literally stepping out of your body; simply imagine that you are looking through your light body's eyes and feeling yourself standing where it stands. Keep your attention there for as long as possible.

Don't try to move from that spot. Simply allow your consciousness to look around the room from that one spot. If you move before you're ready, you will wind up back in the physical and have to begin the process again. Once your consciousness is stable, you can will your light body anywhere. You don't have to walk out a door or move through the ceiling or walls. You can *will* yourself wherever you want to go, and you'll be there.

When you're done exploring, get back to where you made the light body, then allow your consciousness to head back to your physical body, by simply willing it in your mind. Dismantle your light body by imagining it dissipating into nothingness, or you can imagine the light body being reabsorbed into yours so you retain all your energy and have an even better memory of all you did.

Technique #2: Travel by Meditation. Find a quiet place where you will not be disturbed and where you don't have to worry about someone walking in on you. This concern can hamper your ability to relax. Quiet is very important for you to practice, especially as a beginner successfully. Over time you can project regardless of the surrounding noise.

Make sure your body is nice and warm when you astral project. If it's too cold, you cannot remain in your meditative state unless you're an advanced practitioner. Cover up with an afghan or something and wear loose clothing or remain in the nude beneath the covers. You may sit up or lie down. If sitting, keep your spine straight to allow energy flow. If lying down, ensure you're practicing at a time when you will not fall asleep, so you can project. Be able to continue in this position for at least an hour without feeling uncomfortable.

Shut your eyes, take slow, deep breaths, and exhale all tension and stress out of our body. Do a slow body scan and get rid of all pressure by imagining a wave of relaxation undoing those knots. Progressively relax your whole body from head to toes.

Once you are totally relaxed, enter your altered state of consciousness by counting down from ten to one using the visualization technique we covered in an earlier chapter. Go as deep as feels natural to you and do your best to keep your mind from wandering to mundane stuff. If you don't, you'll just fall asleep. You can avoid this by saying a mantra or word repeatedly while imagining an object as simple as a square or triangle or whatever shape you want. This way, your mind has something to focus on.

When your body goes numb, resist the temptation to move or twitch or flex anything. Notice the feeling or urge to do so and then release it. Let your mind drift on to seeking depth: no sight, no sound matters. This is the point where you'll feel a swaying sense on the inside or where you'll see much colored lights on the screen of your inner eyes. Do not attempt to force yourself out of your body. Just let your consciousness separate from your body when it is ready. Your only job is to be as detached from everything as possible, keeping control of the whole experience with a forceless will.

It will soon occur to you that you can see the room around you or that you can see another environment near you. This means you've astral projected. Remain there for a moment and make mental notes of all you can see and hear, so you can check its veracity later. When you move, only to find yourself back in your body, simply will your consciousness back out to the place where it was. Don't try to go to some other place for now. Let it go back to where it knows. You might need a few more sessions to gain the ability to take your astral body wherever else. Just give it time.

Ready to end your projection? Move your consciousness back to your physical body by becoming aware of it. Count forward from one to ten, gradually returning to normal consciousness. Slowly allow yourself to become cognizant of the body, noticing your head, neck, chest, belly, thighs, calves, and feet. Gently flex your feet and hands as you open your eyes, nice and slow. Don't get up too fast. Give yourself time to get used to the physical.

Remember: You must journal your experiences. Notice what worked, what went wrong, and how you can adjust during your next session.

Chapter Six: Building Your Sacred Space

If you truly intend to practice magic, you need to create a sacred space dedicated to your practice. Having this space primes you to move to a state of mind that allows you to express the power within you. You know when you're there that you must clear your mind and allow the divine to come through you.

Your Altar

Think of your altar as your sacred workspace, where you perform your magical rituals. The altar is also where you keep all the tools you need for your magical practice, and all things that represent the purpose or theme of the rituals you conduct. Most religious, magical, and spiritual ceremonies involve the use of altars. Humans have always set up altars for their religious and spiritual ceremonies, across religions and cultures, whether it's a pile of bricks, a table set in the center of the room, or in a corner.

You can choose an altar that is practical and simple, or one that is extravagant and a lovely sight. At the end of the day, your altar, which is a table or a platform, is the place you treat with the utmost honor, devotion, and respect. You allow nothing or anyone to desecrate it. You can place both functional and symbolic items, representative of the deities and spirits you honor. At your altar, you meditate, chant, say your prayers, cast your spells, and do any other rituals you must.

When you keep the altar sacred and pure, you are basically keeping an open door for the energies you work with to come through and concentrate in that area, working with you as you set your intentions, perform your rituals, or celebrate your manifestations.

You will find the altar to be of many benefits to you for expressing gratitude for your blessings, exploring your creative side, seeking guidance, fostering spiritual growth, and going on a deeper and deeper exploration of your true self.

You may wonder if an altar is necessary for your practice. First, you must answer a few questions about magic. Is it something you're genuinely interested in? Do you find that you're usually performing your rituals in a specific room or area? Do you find that your decorations change along with the seasons? If your answer to even one of these questions is yes, then you just might find having an altar will be of immense benefit to you. However, you don't have to have one. In the end, it's your choice. You know within you whether you must have an altar.

Creating Your Altar

You must first decide on the location of the altar. Where do you want it to be? Ideally, it should be a part of your home where you will not be disturbed, whether indoors or outdoors. You must also consider the type of surface you intend to use and where it would be most ideal for you to carry out your magical work in your chosen space.

The location of the altar can also depend on the main intention behind your magical rituals. For instance, if you're working with Aphrodite, the goddess of love, then you might find it best to set up your altar in your bathroom or your bedroom. If you're working with deities or spirits for abundance, then it would make sense to place your altar in the dining room, or in the kitchen, as a symbolic representation of feasting, abundance, warmth, security, and all else tied in with your intentions.

You need not use any super fancy material to serve as the surface. Whether it's a plastic table, a concrete slab, a wooden plank, or whatever, you just want it to be somewhere; it will not be disturbed. Pay special attention when you clean out the space where your alter will be, so you get rid of negative or old, stagnant energy before it's all set up. You may burn sage while chanting a mantra to clear out unwanted energy.

Next, you must think about what goes on your altar. For starters, if it is your desire, you could place an altar cloth over your altar. This clarifies it to your mind and all present energies this space is designated for holy work. You can also take advantage of the magic of color by choosing a color that represents your intention and will supercharge it. If your magical ritual is for love, try a deep red. If it's for abundance, see how green works to supercharge your ritual. If you seek the peace of mind, try a nice calming blue. For increased spiritual growth and insight, seek lavender or purple.

Besides the altar cloth, you will need objects that represent the four elements and/or the four directions. Using lit candles will represent the element of fire, and the south; using a bowl of water will represent the west, and the water element; feathers can represent air and the east, while a bowl of salt (or Earth) will represent the north, and the Earth element. You may choose other objects to signify these things; remember that your practice is personal. Follow your intuition, and you won't be steered wrong.

Another object you will need is a representation of the deity or spirit with which you'll be working. Black candles are used to work with God's energy, while white candles are used to work with Goddess energy. You can also use statues, symbols, pictures, or whatever else you intuitively feel is most representative of the deity.

Use crystals and special stones to supercharge your magic and amplify your intention. Various crystals have various purposes, so pick something that will serve your intention and increase your magical work success. To take things up a notch, consider lighting incense and making use of essential oils. These will help you set the mood for your magical work and will cause you to be more grounded by working with your sense of smell. They also are very effective in cleansing bad energy.

Finally, you'll need your journal, or a grimoire, or a book of shadows. In this book, you'll have records of all your rituals, spells, recipes, lunar events, and notes on your experiences or insights you received during or after performing your ritual. Set your journal on your altar, so it's easy to use, and its intention is very clear for magic only.

If you're working with a deity, or spirit, or god, or the soul of a dearly departed one, then you should have objects representative of them on the altar. Do the proper research so you know the best symbols to use and so your rituals feel very authentic to you.

Care for Your Altar

Each day, you must make sure you work with your altar, or that you work around it at least. Light up the candles. Do you have flowers there? Change them as soon as they die and keep the water fresh. Make sure everything remains in its place. Treat it as you would a live, sacred deity. You often invoke a lot of energy from your altar, so you want to make sure that it's always just right and that you don't ignore it either.

Whenever you invoke a deity, it is in your best interest to do something that shows your gratitude to them. You could present them an offering from nature, or you could bake something that is made with herbs that deity resonates with. If you can't do that, you could sit for a few minutes, simply saying "Thank you" repeatedly, and feeling appreciation for them wash over you.

Cleansing Your Altar's Space

Your altar will give you a form of focus, so you can channel your spiritual intentions as pure as possible. It allows you to do your prayers and affirmations with a sense of clarity and with clean, potent energy. It should be the place you go when you need to recharge, recalibrate, and ground yourself anew. Therefore, it's so important that you consecrate the space you choose and keep it holy.

To cleanse the area, you must first sweep it. Once it's nice and clean, you can then begin the process of smudging. Smudging involves burning an herb with cleansing properties. The most favored of all herbs for cleansing is the sage. In the process of living life each day, energy can gather and stagnate, and this stagnant energy is of no good to you when you're practicing your magical rituals. Smudging is a very ancient ceremony where plants like tobacco, sage, and sweetgrass are burned. This smoke gets rid of all negative ions in the space, and then it allows blessings to flow through the environment so things can become new and dynamic again. Smudging is simply giving your space a reboot and re-energizing. It's a process that even removes any bacteria that might be in the air.

To smudge your sacred space, you'll need sage. This symbolizes the element of earth. When burned, its smoke symbolizes the element of air. You'll also need an abalone shell in which to place the sage or whatever holy plant you're working with, so you can burn it safely. The abalone shell represents the element of water. If you don't have access to a shell, you may simply hold the smudge stick with your fingers.

You've obviously got to have a box of matches or a lighter. This will represent the element of fire. A feather will be needed to represent the air element. When you don't have a feather, you can simply wave your smudge stick about, allowing the smoke to represent the element of air.

It helps to have sacred drums or sacred percussive music, which will represent the heartbeat. If you don't have access to drumming music or drums, you can simply make a clear intention about your heartbeat, and then imagine there is drumming going on. You must trust in magic to create the sounds for you.

What to Do When There's No Room

You may live in a home where there's barely enough room for you to have an altar, or there are too many people in every room, and it just means you will have no privacy. If the former situation is your case, then don't worry about having a dedicated space to perform your magic. This can be to your advantage.

Even if the only space you have to yourself right now is your bed, you can make the process of clearing the energies and setting up all your magical tools a part of your ritual. Think of it as preparing your mind to deal with the mystical, even as you prepare your bed for the same thing. If you're worried about using your bed, especially when using candles, then you can simply clean a good spot on the floor and then set up your tools there.

If you live in a home with just too many people, consider performing your rituals during the night when everyone else has gone to bed. You can also simply find a suitable spot outside for you to set up your altar and begin your magical rituals.

If you have no other options, then remember that magic is magic. It is not limited by the presence or absence of an altar. You can still perform your rituals and do your meditations. If you feel that having an altar will prepare you, then you can imagine that where you are is holy ground, for it truly is. You can also hold on to an object, like a crystal or a stone, and allow that be what you use to center you and ground you so you can work with the energies you require as you do your magic.

Magic that won't work without the presence of all these tools and altars aren't magic to begin with. The purpose these things serve is to help put you in a state of mind where you can easily focus on your intentions. The more you practice — particularly meditation — the more you'll realize that wherever you are in the moment is a sacred space. The divine is not limited by the physical. Remember that.

Chapter Seven: The Tools of the Craft

There are certain devices that, while not necessary, can help the practitioner of magic. When you set up your practice, begin with the devices that have historically proven to be very effective for others who began their magical journey before you. Then adjust as needed, as you find a magical philosophy that matches your personality and lifestyle. Try to remember that there is no such thing as a right or a wrong way of going about your magical practice. Simply go along with what you feel in your soul to be perfect for you.

Be open to experimenting with new tools, yourself, or others who share a love for and understanding of magic.

Magical tools often correspond with the four elements and the four directions.

- **The North/The Earth:** Represented by the Pentacle and Salt. Meaning "To Know."
- **The South/Fire:** Represented by the Blade and the Candle. Meaning "To Dare."

- **The East/Air:** Represented by the Wand and Incense. Meaning, "To Will."
- **The West/Water:** Represented by the Chalice and the Cauldron. Meaning, "To Keep Silent."

Now let's sink our teeth into the tools of the magical trade.

The Altar: We've already covered this. It's where you do most of your magical work. On the altar, there is typically a representation of the four elements and the four directions. You can also find pictures of one's ancestors, representations of spiritual beings in the form of a statue or a painting, a censor used for burning incense, an offering bowl, crystals, stones, amulets, and whatever is important to the Magus.

The Athame: This is a ceremonial blade that customarily has a black handle. This dates to the Middle Age grimoire known as the Key of Solomon. You'll also see mention of fit in the 1950 works of Gerald Gardner. The *athame* is for channeling and directing more powerful energies, which are basically etheric fire. Usually, the blade is left unsharpened and will have some iron to keep all evil entities away during a ritual.

It is connected to the element of fire because of the forge's heat. There are traditions that insist the athame is of the air element. However, it is still a powerful tool you can use to make the spirits or elements do your bidding, as it also connotes an air of threat when you wield it during a ritual.

The Bell: This bell is a great tool for clearing out all negative energy in a space or around an object or a person. It also works to prepare the mind, putting it in the headspace for the magical rituals about to take place. The same can be said of any musical instrument used during a ritual. When the bell rings, it grabs the attention of helpful divine entities to fortify your intention and help you see it through.

The Besom: This is a broom, historically known as the witch's broom. This can be a source of inspiration or terror. The old Witches would concoct flying potions using the most dangerous of hallucinatory ingredients, and they would take flight under the influence of their magical potions on their brooms. The broom is a tool and a symbol for cleansing, physically and magically, and is used to purify the sacred space for your ritual. If you put it above your new home's door, it will keep out all negative entities and all bad luck. However, as you move to a different home, you must have a fresh broom. Do not carry the old one with you.

The Book of Shadows: This is a book that has been made by hand, and is filled with every recipe, spell, ritual, and mystical knowledge from a coven of witches or from a solo practitioner of magic.

The Boline: This tool has a white handle, and it's a favorite of witches and gardeners as well. It has serrations on the inner blade that are very helpful for making wands. The sharp exterior edge does a great job of cutting plants and dicing them into bits.

The Chalice: This vessel contains spiritual energy and usually holds wine within it. When the practitioner offers a guest to drink of this wine, it is a symbolic invitation to partake in the blessings that accrue from the ritual. In Wicca, the male athame is inserted into the female chalice to symbolize sexual intercourse, or the "Great Rite." This is balancing the masculine and the feminine and the energy of procreation and regeneration.

The Candles: These are perfect for giving your magical work a good charge. Historically, the flame is regarded as a spark of life force or source energy. It symbolizes the divinity of communication, and it is the fire element itself, which brings about spiritual and physical change. The candle is your life energy and mental power extended, allowing you to project your will into the universe and to your spirit guides for it to be manifested.

The Cauldron: Historically, the cauldron was a cast-iron pot that our ancestors used for cooking. In some parts of the world, the cauldron is still used for cooking. This is a very vital magical tool. When performing scrying rituals burning rituals that lead to transformation, and when directing our will toward specific intentions, the cauldron represents all the elements. Its round shape is a representation of the earth or mother nature. Its three legs represent water, as the maiden, or the mother crone, or the phases of the moon. The fire beneath it is revered for its transformational power, and the smoke or steam that rises off the cauldron represents the air element.

The Censer: This is where incense is burned. There are people who use a thurible instead. The smoke you see from the burning incense will take your spiritual messages and intentions to the divine beings you have chosen to work with. Many kinds of incense have specific ingredients that help with certain rituals, so you will need to do your homework to discover which kind you should work with at any point in time. A censer is basically a safe place for you to burn your chosen incense. The thurible is a kind of censer that hangs from a chain you can carry around or that lets you swing the incense back and forth as you cleanse your space.

The Clothing: Not just any clothing. This is the ritual attire, which is very vital for a lot of magic practitioners. Historically, witches would put on dark, black cloaks at night so the public eye would not fall upon them and so they would not be persecuted for practicing their magic.

You will need to have an article of clothing – be it a shirt, a tunic, skirt, hat, or a special pair of gloves or pants – which you only ever use during the performance of rituals. In time, you will find that wearing this item will put you in a magical frame of mind as soon as you've got it on, so you don't have to spend time meditating or breathing, trying to find the perfect frame of mind to begin your great work.

The Crystals: There are all sorts of crystals, but each is powerful for bringing about the change you seek in your life. Crystals remind the magician when she wears or carries them around of her intention and what she intends to see come to pass in her life. The subtle energies that emanate from the crystals merge with your energy and will assist you with anything you're doing in life. They will often have the property of the elements of life. For instance, agate portrays the earth, aquamarine represents water, citrine suggests fire, and lepidolite means air.

The Divinatory Items: These items allow you to gain rare insight into whatever burning questions or matters you have on your mind from a supernatural standpoint. There are tools to divine the answers. These include runes, oracle cards, animal omens, alomancy (also called "spilled salt"), aeromancy (using the weather), ogham, melted wax, dowsing, tarot, spirit boards, ashes, crystals, I Ching, numerology, pyromania, astrology, bibliomancy (books) and so much more.

The Grimoire: This is a record of all things magical, including your experiments, your thoughts, and the clear guidance you have received on how to carry out your rituals. Whether yours or another's, the grimoire will often have precise instructions that show you how to invoke an angel or a demon, how to gain and develop your spiritual powers, and how to perform divination properly. Grimoires have been in circulation throughout Europe ever since the Middle Ages, despite the Church's desperate undertaking to burn all things it considered occult.

Back in those times, it was vital for the practitioner of magic to keep their grimoires well-hidden to avoid being persecuted by the Christian church or burned at the stake. We've come a long way since then, and you can now safely have your grimoire wherever is most convenient for you — preferably right on your altar so that you can easily refer to it during your rituals as needed.

The Offering: You'll need an offering bowl. It doesn't matter what material it is made of. The whole point behind this is to put in offerings that are symbolic and will be appreciated by the deity you're working with.

The Oils: Magical oils make your rituals more potent than ever and will help you remember your goals as you perform your magical exercises. You can use these oils for candle magic, meditation, charge your amulets and other tools, spiritual cleansing, making potions, anointing or healing another, and more. You want to ensure you only use the natural oils and stay away from the chemical ones in every corner of the market these days. You want to make sure your magical oils are natural, essential oils.

The Pentacle, or the Pentagram: Across every ancient culture, from Greece to Egypt, the Latin America Mayans to India, and even China, the five-pointed star or the pentagram has always been viewed as a powerful, potent, and ever-present symbol in the history of humanity. You'll discover it etched on caves from the Neolithic era. You'll notice it in drawings from ancient Babylon, showing Venus on its astrological journey. You'll find pentagrams in Hebrew scripture as well.

Whether you call it the pentacle or the pentagram, they mean the same thing. It is a talisman that every magic practitioner would do well to own if they can. If you wear a pentacle, it protects you from bad luck and negative experiences. It will chase away all evil entities and bring the good ones close to you so that they're willing to aid you in all your endeavors. The pentacle also represents all five of the classical elements: Earth, Water, Fire, Air, and Ether (or spirit). Usually, the one solitary point on the pentacle is placed upwards, representing the human form, and the entire star is usually within a circle, which represents protection and a mastery of all four elements by the spirit of the wearer.

The Scrying Bowls: These scrying bowls give you with spiritual insight and allow you to see visions. You can use them with water, fire, smoke, or any other substance on hand.

The Staff: Where it's not legal for you to use blades, you can use a staff instead. With the staff, you show you are connected to the earth. The staff has been used for the centuries by Shamans, who are very connected themselves. In certain spring ceremonies, it is also used to wake the Earth, the Great Mother, from the slumber of winter, by gently beating it on the ground. You may decorate your staff and charge it with magical symbols, runes, crystals, amulets, oils, and herbs. It can also be manipulated in place of a wand.

The Wand: This is a thin rod you hold in your hand, generally made of wood, crystal, ivory, stone, or precious metals like silver and gold. The magus uses the wand to channel energy as needed. The athame is often used to issue commands, the wand is used in a much gentler manner to encourage all entities and energies to grant your intentions peacefully. Wiccans see the wand as a representation of the air element. Other traditions see it as a symbol of fire instead.

The wand is used to point your attention towards whatever you want to will into the world. It communicates clearly what your Will in any situation. Use it to channel healing energy to others or to yourself. You can manipulate the wand to implant a set purpose into a talisman, crystal, candle, amulet, or any other magical object you're working with. With it, you can softly encourage spiritual energies you desire to come to your aid. You can use your wand for fishing out any energy blockage in a place or in the body and remove them. Or you can use it to open your chakras, or those of another; create portals which will connect you to otherworldly realms, and even pass along your will to your helpful spiritual guides.

The Most Powerful Tool of All

One tool determines the effectiveness of all other tools. You can't find it in a shop, nor can you buy it, I'm afraid. This tool isn't even it. Well, what is "it?"

In a word: You!

While every magical tool has its importance and possesses its very own vibration, which continues to grow stronger and stronger with prolonged use, your spirit is most vital in your rituals. These tools are lifeless in and of themselves. What powers them is simply your Will and intention, your constant use of and practice with them.

It is always important that, you perform your rituals from a place of pure love and true compassion for everyone else, with the intent that no harm comes to you or anyone involved directly or indirectly.

Create techniques that work well for you, though they might differ from what others are engaged in. Remember that you have your own special path, your own True Will. When things do not turn out as you'd like, or your intention doesn't come to pass in the ways you'd prefer, or as at the time you'd have preferred, what you've got to do is keep adjusting as your intuition leads you to, until you become better. Continue practicing until your practice becomes a habit you engage in on autopilot, wherever you are, no matter the circumstances. Again, magic is not dependent on objects or environments. True magic lies within you.

I leave you with this final, very important note before we move on to the next chapter: Do not fall into the trap of ascribing power to the items outside of you. They are tools and nothing more. The hand has the authority, not the hammer in hand. It will only do as the hand directs it. If the hand does nothing with the hammer, then the hammer is just another useless thing. Do not give away your power to that which is lifeless. Take responsibility for your life and your manifestations.

Chapter Eight: Preparing for Ritual

Practicing magic effectively means that the magician must participate in some form of ritual to give his intentions clear direction and have a distinct focus on what energy to draw and where to direct it.

What's A Ritual?

It is basically a process or a whole sequence of various activities, which include actions, words, gestures, and objects. These exercises are carried out in a sacred, consecrated space and will always follow a specific order.

They are more common than you think. Even singing the national anthem before a football match is a ritual on its own. Typically, it will have formality to it, and it's often rooted in ancient traditions. No one strays from the set sequence, as there are rules that must be followed to the letter. You'll also find that most of them involve a lot of symbolism and performance as well.

There are all sorts of rituals, from religious sacraments to worship rites, purification rites to rites of passage, atonement rites, coronations, dedications, marriages, presidential inaugurations, funerals, and more.

Elements and Components of Rituals

Formalism: They are often set according to strict codes that give no room for improvisation or deviation. The element of formalism shows up in the way the magician and other participants speak during the sacred event. There's a certain intonation, series of words, volume, and order, inducing a mood of magic and acceptance in all who partake.

Traditionalism: They are often based on ancient, age-old traditions. It is important to remain true to the original form of the ritual as much as possible for it to have meaning and to achieve the desired aftermath.

Consider the well-known Thanksgiving dinner, a good old-fashioned American ritual, with its origins from America's Puritanical settlement.

Invariance: All rituals leave no room for alteration. There is a deliberately orchestrated series of movements or choreography. It will compel you to discipline your body to mold your mind into a condition suitable for magic.

Rule Governance: They have rules by which they are governed. Like the element of formalism, rules instill certain norms and checks to make sure that all behavior conforms to the mood of the group. The guidelines clarify it what is acceptable or not.

Sacrifice: Magic, by its very definition, has rituals that are supernatural in nature. When working with particular deities, angels, demons, or other entities, there will usually be a need for sacrifice. This does not necessarily mean that one needs to make blood sacrifices or anything of the sort; it can simply be enough that you make sure there are symbols that represent you choosing to give - or "sacrifice" - and you're mindfully allowing the forces that need to work on your behalf the freedom to do so.

Performance: They are often like an actual stage performance. It has a spirit of theater, and rightly so, considering that every element and object used during one is symbolic, representing something else. They all have meaning, which must be enacted by the magician.

The Importance of Rituals

Whether it's your secular life or your sacred life, they matter. Even the way you begin your day, the way you get to work, and the way you handle holidays or resumption of your duties are rituals. They connect the past to the present and the present to the future. They perceive continuity and bring about order to our lives.

Magical rituals take you away from the secular and mundane to the magical space. All the sequences involved in one work hand in hand to generate the energy you need and then release that same energy with laser-like precision to help you achieve your goal.

The human is a creature of habit, so not surprisingly, we find a lot of safety and comfort in our rituals. We have a sense of dependability and can trust that things will work out a certain way, regardless of the apparent chaos in the outside world. They let you know where you belong in all the seemingly randomness of life.

Embedded in them are a lot of history and cultures, all of it reflecting the beliefs of magicians from the past till now. Think of it as a spiritual manual which has the blueprint of the magical life. As a magic practitioner, you have a goal or a wish you want to be reflected in you by the universe. All the elements, and the words, choreography, environment, and objects used, have the singular purpose of raising your energy and channeling it towards the thing you desire, making you become part and parcel of the present magic.

For the Magus, they are all about fulfilling her True Will. As she conducts her ritual, she marries the fleeting and the lasting together in the here and now. She melds into the divine and brings the timeless and unseen by the masses right before her very eyes.

They allow you the space you need to channel even more energy than you could through any other means and then actively send that energy out to fulfill your bidding.

Preparing for Your Ritual

As a magician, one of the first things you must do is to take care of your immediate surroundings. If you don't have that much sorted out, how do you plan on directing the energies and forces of nature? You must make sure that your space, as it is, is suitable for magical work.

Wherever you choose to have it will affect the results you get. So, it's best to make use of spaces that allow for energy flow. Consider doing yours outside, or imagine that the energy of nature flows unimpeded to the space you're using indoors. Ideally, performing them in nature is a good way to go, as it allows you and other participants to recognize that we're all woven into the same tapestry.

You may find that you're a bit limited in your choice of location. Do not let that affect you. Simply work with what you've got. You want to make sure that the space you choose can hold you and anyone else who's participating in it.

You want to perform yours in a space you have saged and consecrated for the purpose. You don't want interruptions, distractions, or anything that could take away from the quality and the focus required. You will also want to make sure there are no cell phones or tablets nearby. To set the mood, you can use aromatics, trinkets, and things of that nature.

All seasonal rituals will usually have symbols and decorations that represent that particular season. For instance, an Ostara ritual would benefit from fresh blossoms. You want to choose good music, appropriate incense, and the objects that match the theme of yours. These will play a huge part in affecting your perception, putting you in a magical frame of mind.

As for personal preparations, you must be in the right frame of mind. The same goes for everyone else who joins in. The reason is that everyone's thoughts and emotions will combine, and this energy will feed the group. Everyone must set aside all unimportant and mundane problems and concerns so everybody has the same focus and intention.

Ritual baths before the ceremony are helpful, as they can help cleanse any lingering, old, undesired energy and keep that from tainting your intention. You'll want to add salt to your bathwater - as salt symbolizes purification. You could also add natural, essential oils. If you can, bathe in the ocean, or a lake or stream. Otherwise, don't sweat it. Just take a bath where you can before yours begins.

If you're performing one with others, you'll want to be in a circle. This represents that each person present is responsible for the events that take place, and everyone is equally relevant. All participants must be very clear in their understanding about the reason you've all gathered and should be ready, willing, and able to give of their energy, physically and psychically, so the purpose of it will be fulfilled. If anyone cannot keep their energy positive and clear, then it would be in the interest of all for them to leave. The last thing you need is a weak link who will derail it.

Finally, all ritual objects and tools must be cleansed beforehand. Energetically charge each object so it performs its designated task. Gather every tool you need, and only then should you cast a circle.

The Progression of the Ritual

Every ritual has a progression, with each step being exactly where it is in the sequence of events for a very good reason. Think of them as well-structured plays. You don't want to mess with the orders of the scenes; otherwise, all meaning will be lost.

They all have their very specific beginnings, which will involve creating the sacred environment in which remaining events will occur. The start of your ritual will dictate how the rest of it will go. It takes every participant to the mental space they need to be, transporting them to the point between the physical and the spiritual, where all is one. It unites everyone in spirit and mind so they can focus on the intention for which all have gathered with one collective heart.

At the start of it, you can have all participants breathe together at the same pace while linking their hands and calling on all deities and angels that need to be present. If you're a magician practicing solo, you will need a moment to pray or meditate and invoke the circle.

Once you've arrived at the point of harmony, what happens next will depend on the goal. You might weave spells, sing, drum, or dance. You could sit in meditation, or visualize, engage in divinations, or even enact a symbolic event. Whatever you do choose should match with your intention.

Remember that the more you involve the senses, the more you will raise the energy needed to make yours a success. This means burning incense, incorporating music, and things of that nature. You will notice that as the energy rises, the drumming or chanting might become faster and louder. This is a good thing.

The end of it is just as important as the beginning. It helps to have a solid finish, one that will direct all magicians' attention back to the regular, mundane things of life. If it doesn't have a proper ending, it will be like a bad cliffhanger in a TV show. The participants will have a sense of incompleteness, and the intention of it may remain unfulfilled.

You must have an end to your ritual, which includes acknowledging your desire has been accomplished and releasing all spirits and deities summoned to assist you with it. Also, all participants must ground themselves. When done, deconstruct your circle, say a prayer of thanks, or end with a chant. Each participant must accept the knowledge it is complete and that the intention is sent forth and shall not return unfulfilled.

Chapter Nine: Performing Purification

Staying clean and pure is very vital for every magical act. This is why there are purification rites.

Purification

Purification is the process of setting yourself free and clear of all that is unclean, especially before you do anything magical or work with deities and spirits. You must make sure that you are clean, in mind, and in the body.

Purification doesn't just apply to you; it applies to the objects you use during a ritual and the space you're conducting it in. Historically, the phrase "cleanliness is next to godliness" has been used to explain that being pure is something you do not skimp on during your magical practice.

A lot of rituals insisted on cleanliness, even long before the germ theory was discussed. Eastern religions have always valued purity, both physical and mental. To be impure during a ritual was always a taboo. An added benefit of purification practices is that everyone knows they're not at risk of contracting something from the other person. Impurities range from trash, bodily fluids, and waste to immoral behavior within the context of your magical beliefs.

Purification is almost the same thing as banishing, except it's a lot more rigorous, in that you must prepare not just your temple but yourself to carry out your rituals. According to Crowley, magicians of old often went through very arduous purification methods, fasting, abstaining from sex, going on very special diets, making sure the body remained clean and tidy, and doing a series of very complex prayers.

Don't worry about partaking in all of this, though, because Crowley also says that there's no longer any need for all of that to purify yourself. You can simply set an intention, will yourself to be pure, and that's the end of the matter. This is how you can keep your mind and body pure from all things that would interfere with your spiritual practice. Crowley writes in Magic, Book IV:

The point is to seize every occasion of bringing every available force to bear upon the objective of the assault. It does not matter what the force is (by any standard of judgment) so long as it plays its proper part in securing the success of the general-purpose [...] We must constantly examine ourselves and assure ourselves that every action is really subservient to the One Purpose.

For Crowley, it was enough to participate in symbolically relevant rituals like bathing and robing. Taking a bath is a symbol that shows you have removed everything that is not supportive of your one intention. Putting on your robe also shows that you're donning all that is good and supportive of your intention.

Banishing

Banishing is a ritual that removes all spiritual influences that should not be in the ritual space, from spirits to negative, stagnant energies. A lot of banishing rituals exist, but you can keep it as simple as needed.

Before you cast a circle — which means to draw a magical circle around you and your participants that will channel your energies better and keep you protected — you want to perform this to sanctify the magical area. Banishing is literally casting all unwanted entities and energies away from your space. You'll want to do your banishing as regularly as possible so that your altar and magical work area remain free and clear of negativity and impurity, so you can practice your magic and spells.

Crowley suggests that you do a general banishing and keep it short. Of course, other ceremonies are more elaborate, requiring you to banish everything negative, according to its name. Crowley says you should do your banishing ritual at least once a day, as a true Thelemite.

Staying Clean

You cannot afford to be an unkempt, untidy, and dirty person as a magician in the spirit of cleanliness and purity. You must learn to take care of your things and yourself to the best of your abilities.

All outfits used for magical purposes must be kept clean. You, yourself, must make sure that you're physically clean before you put on these clothes or begin your rituals. Bathe in salt water. Wash your magical apparel in salt water. Cleanse all your crystals, amulets, wands, and other objects using salt water, and with the intention that only positive, helpful energies are imbued in them all.

If it seems to you like overkill, think about how important it is to you that every ritual you do, every intention you put forth, not be a total waste of your time at best, or attract the wrong results and the wrong entities at worst.

Crowley's Lesser Banishing Ritual of the Pentagram

The Lesser Banishing Ritual of the Pentagram, also known as LBRP for short, is a magical ritual used by the Golden Dawn order and is now very popular in modern-day occultism. It is often considered a nonnegotiable starter of all magical work, and so important that as a member of the order of the Golden Dawn, you are taught this first (other than other initiation rituals) before you can join the Inner Order.

The Lesser Banishing Ritual of the Pentagram is incredibly dynamic. It requires gestures, calling out particular power words, visualization, evocation, prayer, and the clearing and preparation of a magical work area to allow you to perform more magic or simply do your meditations.

The point of this ritual is to banish any, and all impure forms, any entities about chaos, and all that doesn't perfectly represent the five classical elements of magic. You will need to use your wand to trace pentacles in the air and then draw on the power of divine entities' names. You'll also need to invoke all spiritual forces in charge of all the elements to keep guard over the circle and keep it fortified.

The Lesser Banishing Ritual of the Pentagram and the Qabalistic Cross have certain basic parts that are credited to Eliphas Levi, a French occultist. The origin of the text was a Jewish prayer traditionally said before going to bed. Of course, this is noted by Rabbi Samson Raphael Hirsch in his book, The Hirsch Siddur (1969). This is how it goes:

In the Name of God, the God of Yisrael: may Michael be at my right hand, Gabriel at my left, Uriel before me, Raphael behind me, and above my head, the presence of God.

Preparing for the Lesser Banishing Ritual of the Pentagram

Certain orders say there is certain magical equipment that will be used to perform the LBRP. However, according to the Hermetic Order of the Golden Dawn, there is no need for any equipment. For clarity, the Hermetic Order of the Golden Dawn (Ordo Hermeticus Aurorae Aureae) is a secret society firmly devoted to studying and practicing all things occult, paranormal, and metaphysical, founder by William Wynn Westcott, William Robert Woodman, and Samuel Liddell Mathers, all Freemasons.

That said, here's an approach you might want to consider when you want to carry out the lesser banishing ritual of the pentagram yourself:

- Setting up an altar in the middle of your space where all the instruments that represent the four elements will be placed.

- Putting on a ceremonial robe, like a tau robe, or any other garment you only use during rituals and is only worn by the magician, you.

- Having a ritual sword, or a dagger (the athame will do here) or a wand, if you prefer. You will use these to make gestures of the various points on the Qabalistic cross, and you'll also need it to draw the pentacles and the circle that connects all points.

The Process

According to the Golden Dawn order, the *Lesser Banishing Ritual of the Pentagram* has three parts which must proceed in the following order:

    1. **The Qabalistic Cross**: This can be repeated when you're done with the LBRP. The whole point of this is to create an astral cross using the magus's body. Each point on the cross will match the Sephiroth of the Tree of Life. (The Sephiroth, which are emanations, are the 10 attributes in the Qabalah through which the Infinite shows itself and continues to create all realms, both physical and metaphysical.)

    2. **The Formulation of the Pentacles/Pentagrams**: You will draw a banishing earth pentacle for the purpose of the Banishing Ritual, or you will invoke a pentacle when doing an Invoking Ritual by drawing the pentacle in the air at the four cardinal points, and calling out the name of God that matches each point: YHVH for the East, ADNI for the South, AHIH for the West, and AGLA for the North. In this portion of the ritual, you either banish or invoke all four elements of Air, Fire, Water, and Earth in that order. Finally, you will connect all four of those pentagrams in a circle, which you draw in the air.

    3. **The Invocation of Deities or Archangels**: At this point, you will call upon the Archangels in the right order: Raphael, Gabriel, Michael, and Auriel (or Uriel), asking for their presence while you see them in your mind's eye at each of the cardinal points.

If you so desire, and the Judeo-Christian names are not your cup of tea, then you may replace names of the archangels, God, and the Qabalistic Cross with your own substitutes. For instance, rather than use the Tree of Life, you may turn to the Chakra system of the East instead. Rather than use the names of God, you may chant your mantras instead. All Thelemic magicians will usually call upon the name Aiwass, from the heart, as they carry out the Qabalistic cross. This shows their continued commitment to the intelligent Liber AL vel Legis, or The Book of the Law, which is the main sacred text of the Law of Thelema. The thing to remember is that magic is personal. Remember: Do What Thou Wilt. Find what resonates with you and use that method.

Chapter Ten: Three Methods of Invocation

Invocation involves calling up a deity or divine being or identifying with it. According to Crowley, two things are critical if you're going to have a successful invocation. First, he says, "inflame thyself in praying," and then he says, "invoke often." As you do your prayers, chants, dance, or singing, or whatever you do to invoke the spirits, you raise your vibration to match theirs, making it even more likely that the invocation will succeed. It's not enough to simply chant or pray; what Crowley means by inflaming yourself with praying is to allow it to set you ablaze. Feel the passion burn in your heart and soul. Feel the fire of the divine spark rise within you as you pray, and you will invoke the deity you need to work with.

Next, he says, "often invoke" because, as with all things, practice makes perfect. The more you invoke, the better you will become at entering the right state of mind for the invocation to occur. Each new session will happen easier and faster than the last because you come into your own as you master the process.

It is Crowley's belief there is no other invocation that is more important even than other magical acts, than invoking your very own secret self, or your Holy Guardian Angel if you prefer. When you have invoked your secret self, it becomes that much easier for you to figure out what your True Will is. Here is Crowley's description of the invocation experience in Magic (Book 4, chapter 15):

"The mind must be exalted until it loses consciousness of self. The Magician must be carried forward blindly by a force which, though in him and of him, is by no means that which he in his normal state of consciousness calls 'I.' Just as the poet, the lover, the artist, is carried out of himself in a creative frenzy, so must it be for the Magician."

Invocation essentially involves calling up the qualities of an entity into you. Mostly, invocation rituals are devotional. You must surrender yourself in worship to the deity so the deity can move and live through you and bless you.

Crowley's Three Methods of Invocation

In the book, Magic (Book 4), Crowley talks about the three major invocation classes. He does state that, in essence, all three of these classes or methods are one and the same. However, each method involves the magician identifying herself with the Deity being invoked.

Method #1: Devotion. Here, the magician will attain alignment with the identity of God through loving surrender. The magical will give up all things irrelevant to a life filled with devotion to this deity and will suppress all illusionary aspects of themselves.

Method #2: Calling Forth. The Magician will be aligned in identity with the deity by giving dedicated attention to the desired aspect of himself that he seeks to invoke.

Method #3: Drama. The Magician's identity aligns with the deity's by way of sympathy. It's not easy for the regular Joe or Jane to just abandon themselves completely as an actor would abandon their real selves for the character they play in a movie, but when the magician is able to do this, they will find this method to be the best and the most effective of all three.

Assumption of Godforms

The assumption of godforms is yet another technique that the magician can use to invoke their god or deity. You have only to use all your imagination to assume that you are a representation of the god you want to identify with. See yourself as the sum total of the idea represented by that god.

A great way to achieve this god identification is to arrange your posture so it is characteristic of the god or spirit you wish to invoke and imagine that the body of this god is melding with yours, enveloping yours, so you become the living embodiment of the god. As you do this, you can chant or "vibrate" the name of that god. Wear it upon you. Let the essence of this god permeate you, mind, body, and soul. Behold, you are god.

Be Prepared

I shouldn't have to mention how important it is for you to be prepared before you attempt to invoke any spirit or deity. You must make sure that you are pure in heart, and your ritual space is ready. The last thing you need is to invoke a mischievous spirit or being instead of the spirit you want to work with.

You must be prepared in mind. All things that are not relevant to the invocation must become unimportant to you. Let it all go completely and focus on the goal you must achieve at the moment.

Do your best to make sure that you are of pure vibration. This will mean smudging the area you intend to do your invocation in. You could also chant as you smudge to raise your vibration and put you in a receptive state of mind for the invocation.

Finally, think about what you want to accomplish as you carry out your invocation ritual. Why are summoning this deity? What would you like to accomplish by allowing this deity's qualities to become your qualities as well? Keep that front and center in your mind, with the complete faith and expectation you will succeed, no matter what it is. Begin with a mood of appreciation, knowing, and trusting that your intentions are already fulfilled. This positive, expectant mindset will make certain you get the results you want, and you are not disappointed or steered off course.

Chapter Eleven: The Art of Divination

Divination Defined

Among the many abilities and talents of the adept is the art of divination. The whole point behind it is to get information that would prove useful to you as a magician in your Great Work, where you finally can transcend yourself.

Outside of what goes on between your ears, there are various kinds of intelligence you can connect with to receive the most amazing and accurate insight and information, using symbology. Divination is all about getting that insight from the realm of infinite intelligence.

Divination vs. Fortune Telling

It is not the same thing as fortune-telling. When you meet a fortune teller, they try to predict what will happen to you in the future. This is different in that it's more about learning about the true nature of a situation or a person. It helps you gain insight into people, things, places, and events, and with this information, you can make better choices for yourself.

There is no lack of methods across cultures and traditions all over the world. In the West, occultists commonly turn to astrology, which involves figuring out the influence of the planets on us. Tarot is a 78-card system, with each card possessing its unique meaning. They also use bibliomancy, picking up a book like the Bible, the Bhagavad-Gita, I Ching, or Liber Legis, and opening it to read random spots, and geomancy, which involves randomly marking the earth or a piece of paper so it creates a combo of 16 patterns.

Divination: Subjective and Personal

You cannot consider it to be a perfect science. Crowley himself states in chapter 18 of Magic (Book 4), "In estimating the ultimate value of a divinatory judgment, one must allow for more than the numerous sources of error inherent in the process itself. The judgment can do no more than the facts presented to it warrant. It is naturally impossible in most cases to make sure that some important factor has not been omitted [...] One must not assume that the oracle is omniscient."

In other words, it comes down to how you interpret a symbol. If working with dreams as a divination process, a fire might symbolize a danger to one magus, but to another, it could mean regeneration or a new beginning. The subjective nature of it remains constant, no matter the medium used, whether it's the Tarot, or Runes, or Scrying.

Practical Divination Exercises

Divination by Scrying

Scrying is also known as oculomancy, crystal gazing, or hydromancy. It is a very old practice of revelation. If you've ever seen a movie scene where a gypsy was looking into a crystal ball, scrying is exactly what she was depicting — except real scrying is not about attempting to see the future. No one can see the future. You can only speculate about it based on the information you currently have.

The origin of the word "scrying" is the Old English descry, which meant "to reveal" or "to make out dimly." Scrying is the process of revealing what is hidden with our inner sight or second sight. This site represents our ability to perceive that which we rarely pick up on using just our five senses.

The first mention of scrying was in the 10th century, in the Shahnameh, Ancient Persian writing. When Christianity became a thing, it outlawed all scrying as "devilish." This is funny because, across all cultures, there has always been some form of this art, from the Egyptians who used oil to gain insight to the Native Americans who used smoke to show them mysteries.

With scrying, you can connect with your unconscious mind and with realms beyond the physical. You can get a handle on who you are and why you are. If you are yet seeking your True Will, then scrying will be of immense benefit to you, helping you pinpoint our desires and aspirations.

How to Scry

    1. Find a quiet place where you can work with no interruptions. Set things up to help you relax so you can easily enter a trance. If it helps to have a dim room, then shut the blinds. If it helps to have light, throw open the

shades. You'll want to enter a meditative state before you begin.

2. Know your intention. This way, you're more than likely to get the answers you want to have. Set your intention firmly in your mind.

3. Stare into your chosen medium, whether fire, a crystal ball, a mirror, or water. Your trance state may deepen. This is fine. After some time, you will begin to see images. Shadows, shapes, and silhouettes will form. You may see vague images, or you may see vivid flashes. As you see these things, important dates, locations, and times may come to your mind that relates to your intention. Don't force yourself to see what isn't there. Just let it happen.

4. When you're done, write down everything you saw, and write down the details of how your session went.

It's okay if, at first, you're afraid of what you might see. To deal with this fear, ground yourself so you feel connected to the physical by allowing the energy from the ground to flow up through your feet and the rest of your body, anchoring you. Gently let yourself know just because you see things doesn't mean you've gone mental. Chant the name of a deity who makes you feel safe.

Divination by Dowsing Pendulum

The pendulum shouldn't be overlooked, as it is a powerful way to find the truth about things. It is not only powerful, but it's also easy to create your own at home, with some thread and a key with an eye for you to pass the thread through.

A dowsing pendulum is usually a crystal or a rock you hang on the end of a chain or a string. It gives insight on all levels, whether it's on a spiritual matter, or you must find something that's been buried beneath the floors. It works by connecting you with the Akashic records, which are full of answers to all of life's pressing issues. When you ask a question, your unconscious mind will respond by affecting your fingers nerve endings, and this makes it swing in answer, so your body tells you what you know on the inside.

How to Use the Pendulum

1. Select the right pendulum. Sure, you can make one out of a key and string, but if you need something to help you get into the magical frame of mind, then you should put more thought into what should serve as a proper pendulum. What material do you want it to be made of? To use a crystal, what kind? Think about the power crystal you resonate with the most. You may go to a magic store, hold on to each one available, and see what calls to you the most.

2. Cleanse your pendulum. You want it to be clear of all energy that is stagnant or residual in it. You can cleanse it in salt water, or bury it in the earth for a day, or use a smudge stick. When you intuitively sense it is cleansed, you can then work with it.

3. Develop a relationship with your pendulum. This is a straightforward thing to do, but it will take some time and a lot of commitment, like an actual relationship. You want to learn the language of your pendulum, and you want it to learn the language of your unconscious mind. To make this happen, you must ask it questions. First, breathe deeply so you can be centered and grounded. Next, request support and guidance by praying to your deity, your higher self, or chanting. Ask that you receive the most objective answers and the clearest ones. Finally, ask it a few questions so you can figure out what it means by "yes," "no," and "maybe."

It might say yes by swinging back and forth, not by swinging side to side, or by swinging around clockwise or counterclockwise. To understand what each direction means, you could say it, "Show me yes," then wait to see.

Then tell it, "Show me no," and let it show you. Then ask, "Show me maybe," and watch. Then thank it.

Another approach is to ask questions with objective answers, like, "Am I a man or a woman?" or "Is the sky army green or blue?" or "Am I a parent or not?" Then pay attention to the swinging you get with each question. Make sure always to do this exercise or the previous one because it can change the way it says yes, no, or maybe.

4. Question your pendulum once it's ready for use. Make sure you're comfy in your seat. Make sure your arm is stable and supported at the elbow. Hold it nice and loose between your index finger and thumb. Keep just enough grip to keep it from slipping from your grasp. Suggest the question you want an answer to. You can ask it anything... as long as it's within reason. You could discover whether you should go to an event, see what you feel about something, or decide on a career change. It can help you with everyday problems, relationships, money issues, and spiritual concerns.

Please be wise about how you use your pendulum. Attempt no divination when your mind feels unbalanced or when you're feeling terrible emotionally or physically, as you will get wrong answers. Make sure you're in the right headspace by asking it if it's a good time to proceed.

It should not replace your doctor. If you need health care, please seek a professional. Only practice with it on yourself, not someone else, unless they have given you permission to work with them or on their behalf.

Begin your sessions with an open mind. Get rid of all your biases. If you have a mind that is focused on a subject, this will obviously affect your process.

Know there's only so much it can do for you. You could try it with scrying, runes, or tarot. You can supplement with scrying to check that the information you get from it is true.

Do not be overly reliant on it. It may be great for divination, but the last thing you want to do is make every decision in life-based on which way the pendulum swings. Be careful not to turn it into a crutch. In magic, it is important to be responsible for all your actions and choices and be conscious of your decision-making. Don't ruin your life or someone else's simply because "my pendulum said it was okay." Don't try to pass on your responsibilities to it. Remember, it's a tool. You have the ultimate power, and you alone should take responsibility or blame for your actions as a true Thelemite.

Before each session you should begin by asking:

- Can I ask this question? As in, am I ready for the answer?

- May I ask this question? As in, am I permitted to? This is useful when dowsing or performing divination for someone else. Also, just because they insist you should ask doesn't mean you should ignore it if it tells you no.

- Should I ask this question? As in, is it okay? This is the only time you should use the word "should" in asking questions about your pendulum. Using "should" could cause your biases to affect the answers you get.

Chapter Twelve: More Magical Practices

As we wrap up this book, let's consider even more magical practices you should make a part of your daily magical life.

Consecration

Consecration involves dedicating a space or a ritual tool to a particular purpose. According to Crowley, in Magic (Book 4, chapter 13), "The ritual here in question should summarize the situation, and devote the particular arrangement to its purpose by invoking the appropriate forces. Let it be well remembered that the Oaths of its original consecration bound each object. Thus, if a pentacle has been made sacred to Venus, it cannot be used in an operation of Mars."

The very word consecration connotes "association with the sacred." You can consecrate places, things, and even people. The idea behind the practice of consecration is the devotion of what is being consecrated to one cause, deity, magical function or intention.

Evocation

Evocation should not be confused with an invocation. When you invoke, you call in a deity or a spirit. When you evoke, you call forth the entity. Crowley says, "In invocation, the macrocosm floods the consciousness. In evocation, the magician, having become the macrocosm, creates a microcosm. You invoke God into the Circle. You evoke a Spirit into the Triangle."

There are two distinct purposes for evocation. The first is to assist you in gathering information, while the second is to get the obedience or services of a demon or spirit. Seek the most effective of evocations. You will find in the grimoire on Goetia, an anonymous grimoire on demons, also known as the Lesser Key of Solomon, or the Lemegeton, or Salomonis Regis, compiled in the middle of the 17th century. This grimoire has very clear instructions on how you can safely summon the 72 infernal spirits and set them to do your bidding. You can also evoke angels, gods, and other beings with connections to the Zodiac, planets, and elements.

Magical Formulas

Magical formulas comprise a series of letters, words, or names, which have meanings that represent the magical principles and the depth of comprehension, which are difficult to communicate in any other way. These formulae offer a concise way to share abstract meanings and information using just a phrase or a word. These meanings often relate to a spiritual or mystical process of change. Some of these formulae are IAO, INRI, ShT, LVX, NOX, AUMGN, among others.

Taken at face value, these words do not mean anything in and of themselves. However, upon deconstruction, you'll find that each letter carries a universal idea within it, which is in the system the formula is based on. Also, when you group particular letters together, you can share sequences packed with meaning and are very valuable within the framework of the spiritual system they belong to.

Magical Record

The magician's magical record is a journal in which she can document all magical experiences, events, ideas, and other relevant information to her craft. Having this record can serve to keep the faith and can provide evidence about how effective a magical procedure is. It can help you make sure that all you've learned can be passed on to others long after you're gone. When you note down this information, it's easier for you to gain insights, analyze your progress, and share and learn with other practitioners like you.

For Crowley, you should keep magical records; as he notes in Liber E, you very should record all of your experiments in much detail, right after, or even during your magical performance. You want to make your records scientific and precise. Note the emotions you felt and be honest and sincere be. Note your mental and physical conditions during the experiment, the time and place, and the weather. This information will ultimately prove useful.

Magical Weapons

Magical weapons are used to create the change you seek, which conforms to your True Will. If it is your will to let everyone know what you have learned during your magical practice, then you take the weapons of pen and ink, and you write them down. Crowley acknowledges that sharing your knowledge by writing is a magical act, as is sharing the book in which you have penned your words.

Magical weapons are often very specific, and they're consecrated, and so only ever to be used in ritual or ceremonial magic. There's no rule per se about what makes up a magical weapon or what doesn't, but if you, the magus, consider an object to be a magical weapon, then for all intents and purposes, it is. However, certain magical weapons have a deeper meaning and symbolize other things. For instance, there is the athame or dagger, the holy oil, the wand, sword, oil lamp, graal, thurible, and bell, among others.

Mineral Magic

It is possible to read another's life story from just holding a bracelet of theirs. This is possible because all minerals, from crystals and metals to stones and shells, have within them the vibrations of anything and person they've been in contact with and will often hold on to all those vibrations for quite a long time.

The average person may look at minerals and think them lifeless and static, but the magus knows that you can sense energy from these metals and stones. Crystals have their own life force, as do gemstones and every other mineral of which you can think. When you imprint your intention upon a mineral object, that intention will be retained for years and years. You can also combine minerals with other things so you can strengthen your spells or lengthen how long they last.

Each gemstone has unique properties and can be used in many ways in magic. You can use them as runes, pendulums, or other tools; you can use them for healing the chakras, as a talisman or amulet, for rituals and spells, to increase meditation potency, to amplify the power of consecrated magical weapons and tools, as a gift to gods, and so on.

First, to use minerals like gemstones, wash off all old vibrations, cleansing them in salt water, and visualizing white light cleaning the stones in and out. You may combine these stones together. You can create a talisman for wealth by using tiger-eye stones, and by adding in some hematite, you make sure that whoever uses the talisman can hold on to their money.

Stones and their Magical Uses

- Amber: Protection, both physical and psychic.
- Amethyst: Enhancing meditation, dream recall, soothing emotions, enhancing psychic ability.
- Apache tears: Gives good luck.
- Aquamarine: Increases mental awareness and clarity, allows spiritual insight, boosts creativity.
- Aventurine: Attracts abundance and wealth.
- Azurite: Promotes peace and harmony, excellent for dream magic.
- Bloodstone: Gives courage, strength, healing, and physical protection.
- Carnelian: Increases sexual energy, gives initiative, courage, and boosts passion.
- Citrine: Removes and clears bad energy from other gemstones, banishes all nightmares, boosts your psychic abilities.
- Coral: Boosts feelings of affection, draws love to you, boosts your self-esteem, calms troubled emotions.
- Diamond: Builds trust and commitment, particularly in relationships. It also absorbs and retains vibrations and energies and increases chances of victory while giving strength.
- Emerald: Promotes divination and clairvoyance while boosting growth, healing, and providing emotional and mental balance.
- Fluorite: Boosts your conscious mind's strength and increases your mental skills.

- Garnet Provides protection, draws out kindness, soothes fears, and relieves all depression.
- Hematite: Perfect for grounding and centering yourself, and helps with keeping emotions stable.
- Jade: Boosts prosperity, encourages longevity, increases health and beauty.
- Jasper: Red jasper is amazing when working on love spells as it intensifies passions. Brown jasper is the stone to use for healing. The poppy jasper is best for breaking down all blocks in the body's energy circuitry.
- Lapis Lazuli: Great for children; it opens your third eye and improves your psychic abilities. It works on your higher chakras. The ancient Egyptians knew this was the stone to charge power meridians with.
- Moldavite: This improves your psychic abilities, opens your higher chakras, and speeds up the evolution of your spirit. This stone is extraterrestrial, as it resulted from a 15 million-year-old collision of a meteor with the earth.
- Moonstone: More vivid dreams, increased dream recall, and calmer emotions.
- Obsidian: Perfect for scrying, valued by Hecate, the patroness of witches.
- Onyx: Best for centering and grounding, absorbing and banishing bad energy, and destroying powerful habits.
- Opal: Improves psychic ability, protects, increases your visions, and attracts love to you.
- Pearl: Brings balance to your love life, boosts your femininity, increases your happiness and self-esteem.

- Clear Quartz: The best for retention of information, the amplification of other energies from other stones, the transmission of energy and ideas, and improved psychic awareness.

- Smoky Quartz: Holds your issues until you're ready to have them resolved, improves your endurance.

- Rose Quartz: Heals you emotionally, restores emotional balance, draws friendship and love to you, and amplifies your psychic energy.

- Ruby: Great for stimulating love, passion, and emotions, helps you open your heart to the love of the divine, and increases your vitality.

- Sapphire: Great for improving your knowledge of all things spiritual, this stone connects you with the Divine and gives you insight, wisdom, and prophetic vision. The star sapphire also gives you clarity with your True Will, and it gives you hope.

- Tiger-eye: Increases your self-confidence, which gives you the freedom to seek your own path and follow it. It's also a great stone for abundance.

- Tourmaline: The black tourmaline and green tourmaline are great for healing, cleansing, and absorbing all negative energies and vibrations. The watermelon and pink tourmaline will draw love, friendship, and fulfillment to you. You can also use them to transmit ideas, energy, and messages.

- Turquoise: This stone promotes prosperity, healing, and protection. Use it to soothe all anxiety and tension, physically and emotionally.

Here's a fact to keep in mind: Amber is not actually a stone; it is hardened resin. Lore has it that amber originally came from the tears of the sun as it set. Even now, it's still thought of as firestone or a solar stone. It's a stone most witches use to heal, as it captures all ailments and disease in the same way as it is used to capture insects.

These gemstones are typically available in many grades and qualities. You need not have a large stone for you to conduct your magic. You can simply allow your intuition to let you know the right stone that will amplify the intention you set for the ritual you're about to do.

Consider having magical jewelry made of these gems. They can prove useful for reminding you of your intentions, healing you, and serving as a talisman. Gemstones have always been connected to goddesses and gods and can even serve as offerings during your rituals. Remember that the gemstones you wear will absorb your energy, taking on some of your attributes. For instance, if you're wearing a pearl while you're joyful, it will glow. If you wear it while you feel terrible, it will go cloudy. If you're ever given a family heirloom passed down to you, you must wash it before you wear it to get rid of all unwanted, bad energy.

Conclusion

You have finally arrived at the end of this book, but you must not let your quest for knowledge stop here. It is on you, as a magus, to gather as much knowledge as you can so you can apply it to your craft and get better and better every day.

In your practice of magic, you must remember this: Do what thou wilt. Remember this is the true intent behind everything magical that you do. As you practice magic, remember that what you're doing is simply expressing your True Will in harmony with the universe. This is the only thing that matters, moment to moment.

Be aware that you must practice your craft from a place of love and compassion to all. If you choose to use your powers for evil, if you deliberately engage in magic solely to pull others down, then you must be prepared for the fact that in due time, you will receive the same treatment you've meted out, *and often a hundredfold over.*

Therefore, the wise magus knows in her practice to always remember the Golden Rule: Do unto others as you would have them do unto you. You cannot afford to be irresponsible with the knowledge you now have.

You can learn so many things in so many books about magic, but one thing trumps all books — even this one. It's the knowledge you learn from constant practice, particularly from your meditations. See to it that no matter what, you make meditation a part of your life every day. There are insights you will never glean from the page of a book; you will only experience this as you meditate, and practice Yoga and astral travel.

In your dream state, and in your astral travels, you will learn so much about the true nature of the universe, and you will receive new insight and exercises to practice to take your spiritual journey to the next level. So, you cannot afford to neglect your practice. The more you practice, the more insight you will have, and the more power you will gain.

You may notice that your exercises in this book are mostly kept as loose as possible. This is by design. To work with magical stones, do so based on your intuition. Your soul will guide you on the best methods for you to perform all rituals, from purification and banishment to blessings and divination. The thing about this magical life is that each path is unique. Therefore, you must find the path that resonates the most with you so your practice becomes something you look forward to every day.

Finally, when the supernatural begins to happen around you (and it will if you keep your practice up), please do not fall into the trap of thinking you have "arrived" at a final spiritual bus stop. There is so much more to explore. There is always more beyond where you are. Even if you learn remote viewing or be in two places at once, even if you make prophecies that come to pass no matter what, let none of that wonderful stuff stop you from practicing.

The magical journey is never-ending. Keep diving. And when you get to the bottom of the ocean, dive deeper still.

Part 2: Moon Spells

Unlocking the Hidden Power of the 8 Lunar Phases, Wiccan Magic, and Witchcraft

Introduction

The moon is one of the most majestic objects in the solar system and has inspired respect and curiosity since the early days of human life. This big bright body in the sky carries mysteries and wonders that few can grasp, and its secrets could be the key to unlocking more than we could imagine. This is why the moon is considered sacred to many cultures, and there is a long list of moon Gods and Goddesses across many civilizations.

The different moon phases have made it an everlasting symbol of transformation and time. It has also been linked with birth and death, creation and destruction. This powerful symbol is another reason many cultures have deities associated with the moon.

This book will explore those lunar phases and how each can carry a wave of magic within. You will learn the spells that you can cast during the different phases of the moon. We will cover every step you need to take to conjure the spells you want and explain how you should pair them with the various lunar phases. This guide is ideal for beginners because it presents easy-to-understand tips and hands-on instructions on how to craft those spells.

If you've ever been curious about the other lunar phases and how they could affect spell making, then you have come to the right place. The information you will find here is up to date, and it contains real spells that you can try for yourself. There is no experience necessary when crafting these spells because everything you need will be outlined. All that is required of you is an open mind, and a willingness to try this out.

We will explore all spells, from love to fertility, and how you can craft them. We will also discuss the ingredients and the rituals associated with those spells. If this sounds like something you're interested in, and we are sure that it is, then read on to improve your spell-casting knowledge.

Section 1: Moon Magic Essentials

Chapter 1: Mother Moon: Her Power and Symbolism

You will notice that the moon is often referred to with feminine symbols, and there is an explanation for that. While the sun is seen as representing masculinity, the moon is regarded as the female manifestation of all things. Yet, despite it being a feminine symbol, any gender can associate with and relate to it. Mother Moon is not exclusive of genders or races, and she belongs to everyone.

As we mentioned earlier, many cultures have looked up to the moon and associated Gods and Goddesses with the power and energy that come from it. When you're performing a ritual or spell correlated with the lunar phases, you may call upon one of these deities. In this next part, we will explore the most common deities across various cultures and how people view those higher powers, given the moon. We will also examine how religions associate the moon with feminine energy and consider it a symbol of purity and womanhood. Despite the moon's association with the female menstrual cycle–which we'll discuss in a bit, not all cultures think of the moon as a woman, though the majority do.

Greek Myths

The moon has a very rich background in Greek Mythology. Selene was believed to be the Titan Goddess of the Moon. She drove her moon chariot across the heavens every night, marking the start of a new evening, and is claimed to have had a lunar sphere or crescent on her head as a crown. She is the sister of the Sun God Helios and Eos, Goddess of the dawn. In Greek Myths, Selene is said to have fallen in love with a young king called Endymion, and she bore him 50 daughters, another symbol of the moon's fertility and its association with the feminine archetype. Over time, another woman, Artemis, took over and became the Moon Goddess after Selene. Despite this, Selene has often been considered the personification of the moon itself.

Aztec

In Aztec mythology, the ancient Goddess of the moon was Coyolxauhqui. She was also considered the Goddess of the Milky Way. She is often depicted in Aztec mythology as engaging in a fierce battle with her brother, the God of sun and war. The battle always ends with Coyolxauhqui's horrific death, and her death is often re-enacted in ritual sacrifice across the Aztec Calendar.

Mayan

Ix Chel was the Mayan Goddess of the moon. She was sometimes portrayed as a young and sensual woman who represented fertility, and other times, she was described as an older woman who is associated with death and destruction. Ix Chel was occasionally known as Lady Rainbow.

Christianity

Virgin Mary is often depicted with a new moon, a symbol of peace and illumination. The relationship between Mary and the moon has always been interchangeable. The moon is thought of as an ancient symbol of Mary, the Mother of God, and Mary is a source of light herself, the Mother of God, who is also light.

Polynesian

Sina is the Polynesian deity associated with the moon, and she is one of the most popular deities of that culture. Some say that she resided within the moon itself, and she is the protector of travelers on the road at night. Hawaiian Myth has it that Sina used to inhabit the earth with a husband, but she tired of it, so she left to live on the moon.

Celtic

In Celtic mythology, Cerridwen is the Goddess of the moon and fertility. She was often correlated with knowledge and wisdom and linked to the underworld. She is now symbolized by a white sow in many tales and myths. The sow represents her strength as a mother, and her fertility. She is considered to be both Mother and Crone, and she is often associated with the full moon.

The Moon and the Triple Goddess

As we've mentioned earlier, the moon has often been associated with women and female maturity. The Triple Goddess is the perfect representation of that, and its partnership with the moon has been the cornerstone of several pagan religions. The Triple Goddess was highly revered in Neo-pagan religions and rituals, and she represents a trinity that is the Maiden, the Mother, and the Crone which are the phases of female maturity. Each phase is a separate stage of a woman's life, and each corresponds to a different phase of the moon. In modern pagan traditions (Wicca most of all), the Triple Goddess is the Horned God's female counterpart. But, in Wiccan groups, the Triple Goddess is the only deity worshipped.

The Wiccans view the Maiden as the young woman, virginal, who is yet to awaken. She is about new beginnings and trying new things and the enchantment that comes with that. The Maiden also represents the enthusiasm of youth and youthful ideas. This is why she is associated with the moon's waxing phase when it grows from dark to full moon. This stage and others are worn as crowns by High Priestesses of the Wiccan order. In Greek Mythology, the Maiden is Persephone and was a symbol of purity and the legacy of fresh starts.

The Mother, on the other hand, is maturity and growth. In Wicca and other modern Pagan religions, the Mother is the next phase of a woman's life, and it is one that each must reach. This is when a female gains knowledge and is filled with excitement and fulfills herself sexually, emotionally, and socially. This is also when she's fertile and fecund. The Mother phase is when a woman grows and becomes the optimal version of herself, where she is at the height of her power and prowess. This corresponds to the full moon phase. The Mother roams in spring and early summer, which are her domains. Just like the earth becomes fertile and green in those seasons, so does the Mother. Many Pagan religions and rituals do not see it as necessary for a woman to conceive to assume Mother's role. In Greek Myths, the Mother is Demeter and is the world's source of life and giving.

The last stage of womanhood and the moon is the Crone when a female becomes old. As a hag, the woman has wisdom and is the representation of the darkness of the night. She is also associated with death and destruction. This phase corresponds to the waning of the moon and the dying of the earth. The Crone's domain is winter and its cold, linked with death and the final moments of life. In Greek Myths, the Crone is Hecate, who is wise and all-knowing.

The First Triple Goddess

Diana is an ancient Roman Goddess, also known as Hecate to the Greeks, and is considered being the first of the original Triple Goddess by many. Diana or Hecate was thought to be all three divine Goddesses in one. She is believed to have been represented in triple form even in the early days of her worship, particularly Diana. She was considered Diana the Huntress, Diana as a representation of the Moon, and Diana of the Underworld to represent death.

Hecate was often associated with witchcraft in the early days. Several tales mention a group of witches talking about the Triple Goddess. Interpreting Hecate as the Triple Goddess, which represents the moon phases, has also been present for some time. A Roman Philosopher called Porphyry was the first to make the connection between Hecate or Diana and the three phases of the moon. He described the Goddess beautifully, describing the moon itself as Hecate and claiming she was a symbol of its varying phases, and her powers were drawn from the moon. He likened her three forms to the moon as a figure in white and golden sandals to represent the new moon, and he made similar parallels compared to the other phases of the moon.

The Symbolism of the Moon Phases

The moon's symbolism has been present for millennia, and its phases have been said to affect humans in several ways. Many cultures believe that the moon had a powerful effect on us and can affect human behavior. This is where terms like "moonstruck" developed, which is used to describe people who act strangely. The adjective 'lunacy' comes from "Lunar", Latin for Moon Goddess. In other cultures, individuals believe that the moon is a God who has the power to predict the future. For example, Japanese priests would gaze at a moon's reflection in a mirror because they thought looking directly at it would drive them mad.

The moon's different phases are believed to signify various things, each with a certain set of values and influences.

New Moon: This is the beginning of the lunar phases, and for that reason, since early civilization, the new moon stands for new beginnings. In several cultures, sentinels would watch out for the new moon to herald the start of a new month, and they would report their sightings so the lunar calendar could be planned. The new moon is dark, and this darkness represents a fresh beginning and turning a new leaf. It is time to pick yourself up and set goals for the future. This is when you can plan for achievement over the next moon phases.

Crescent Moon: Now that you have planned for the future and thought about your hopes and wishes, it is time to declare all those things. You get to declare your hopes for the new lunar month and wish for the best. The crescent moon represents femininity and growth and thriving.

Waning Crescent: It is believed that the waning moon signifies losing someone or something with a bad influence on your life, and it is associated with loss and letting go of things. It is also identified with latent periods and meditation. A waning crescent symbolizes getting rid of negative energy in your life and working on becoming better.

Waxing Crescent: This phase represents development and pregnancy. It's about growth and creative thinking. When waxing crescent, you need to think about solutions for the things that trouble you and try to outgrow them.

First Quarter Moon: One week after the new moon, we have the first quarter moon. It represents the importance of having a head start for facing and conquering the challenges you were not prepared for. It is also a symbol of the time to make impulse decisions and act.

Gibbous Moon: When it is this phase of the lunar month, it is time to take a step back and look closely at your life. What are you doing right, and what are you doing wrong? Are you happy? With the Gibbous Moon, you must think about your actions and correct course if needed, without worrying about what has already happened. This phase is also associated with adapting to your current situation.

Full Moon: A full moon represents power and purity. It is the completion of objectives and reaching the peak of your prowess. Therefore, the full moon represents the Mother. A full moon is also a symbol of manifestation for the plans and ideas you have worked so hard for. You might not immediately see the outcome you want, but you're getting there, and you're doing all the right things.

Disseminating Moon: This is the time of the lunar month when you need to be grateful for everything you have and all the intentions that have worked for you. It also symbolizes the importance of being hopeful for the future.

Last Quarter Moon: This phase is about spiritual healing and the advent of the time where you have to move on. The last quarter moon is when you need to let go of past pain and feelings that have caused you to hurt, whether that is toward people or things.

Balsamic Moon: In this final phase, the balsamic moon symbolizes recovery and healing. It is the time to yield and repose, and it is when you should stop reckoning and get in your way. It is time to be at peace. Avoid projecting and taking actions only hurting you. This phase is about stillness and being at peace.

Chapter 2: Lunar Phases: When to Work Moon Spells

Witches and sages have been using the power of the moon for centuries as they understand its immense strength and how they can harness it. They also understand how it can provide them with good fortune, guidance, and success with their spell work. Living your life by the lunar cycle can bring harmony and make you feel happier and more energetic. This is why you need to know the different lunar phases and how to use them to your advantage.

Delving deeper into the topic, you need to understand that you cannot do moon spells at random. Each spell needs to correspond to a certain lunar phase. This is why you always have to consider the moon's current stage before you do these spells. While we discussed an expanded version in the previous section, and the associated symbolism, we will discuss focused stages now. It is generally accepted there are eight main phases of the moon, and it is during those that you should work your spells. There are also special phases of the moon that rarely happen, such as a lunar eclipse, and advanced students of witchcraft can use those for more powerful spells.

You need to believe in yourself and your abilities before you explore these spells because they only work if you believe that you can channel them. As a general concept, before we delve into each distinct phase, know that each corresponds to specific magic that you'll be practicing. For example, at the beginning of a lunar cycle, there is the waxing period (which is defined as the point where the moon is getting larger and growing), and during this, practice positive magic to bring new and good things into your life. Different phases will have specific connotations, which we will explore now.

New Moon

The lunar phases begin with the new moon when it moves to its position between the sun and earth. We rarely see it because it's the dark side that faces us at this stage. Occasionally, it can create a solar eclipse, which happens when it blocks the sun's rays from reaching us, creating a shadow on certain parts of the earth.

This phase of the moon is ideal for exacting a plan or launching a business endeavor. You could also try to gain publicity or introduce your work to the public. It is also great for money spells that will increase your cash flow, and you could try other spells that would lead you to new venture opportunities. Love spells are also common during this lunar phase, and those related to travel and exploration. Remember, the purpose of this is to stop clinging to the past and focus on new goals and dreams. Concentrate on the present and the future with your spells during a new moon, not the past. It's time for magic to drive you to new ventures, rather than dwelling on old pain.

Spells you could try during a new moon include banishing, divination, any magic for fresh starts and new opportunities, self-improvement spells, and curses. The new moon usually lasts for three and a half days from its first appearance--which happens at dawn. The prevalent themes include beauty and abundance.

Speaking of self-improvement, a new moon is also perfect for exploring the darker parts of your soul and trying to manipulate them positively. Each of us has a dark side we often refuse to admit or confront, even when people call us out on it. This is basic human nature, wanting to keep our flaws and the dark sides of our personalities hidden and tucked away. Instead of suppressing those sinister parts yourself, you can use them for good and improve your life during a new moon. Look deep into yourself and find the flaws you know are there but keep buried. Are you good at seeing people's faults and insecurities? Train yourself to utilize that skill to look for people's qualities and good traits. Maybe you can talk your way out of any problem. Think of healthy ways to control that quality, like getting ahead in your job without causing problems or hurting people.

The last thing to remember about a new moon is how it is ideal for setting new plans for the future, as we mentioned when we discussed its symbolism earlier. Set short-term goals during this stage for the upcoming cycle. Plan it by month; how do you wish the next 30 days to look for you? What dreams do you want to work on over this next period? This is great for beginnings, whether it is in love or business or even a social quest.

New moon ritual idea: since this phase of the lunar cycle is about comfort and fresh starts, this simple ritual can be done in your home. Before you begin, you must make sure your space is clean and organized. So, start with decluttering to prepare for the ritual. You could light a candle or burn sage to set the environment, turn on relaxing music, and keep a pen and sacred paper nearby so you can write.

The second step of this ritual is connecting with the Divine energy source you relate to the most, in this case, Mother Moon, or any of the other deities that represent her. Call upon them and honor them in preparation. Now that everything is set, sit down, relax, and write down the details you want for your future and explore your dreams for this next phase of your life. Whether it is a job opportunity, love, or any endeavor, write it down. The next step is reading those desires out loud. This is a crucial step because knowing the things you desire to happen in life, and the feelings that overwhelm you during this step are important for the manifestation.

Finally, after declaring your wishes, sit quietly and meditate. Visualize your hopes and aspirations, becoming real and happening. This ritual can be done on your own, or you could invite your fellow witches to join you.

Waxing Crescent

This second phase of the lunar cycle is called the waxing crescent moon. This is when the moon travels east in the sky. You can tell it is the waxing crescent when you see a small sliver part after the new moon, and it seems to keep growing bigger every night. It is possible at times to see the rest of it, but it will be dark due to a phenomenon known as earthshine, which is when the earth reflects the sunlight to the moon.

In this phase, you need to focus on your intentions and the actions needed to make them happen. You could write down your objectives for the future and read them every day to remind yourself why you're doing this. The waxing crescent is a time of focus and discipline, and preparation for the next step of your plans. During this phase, the moon's glow and power grow, as do yours. So, you want to draw upon this lunar energy and reap its rewards and strength.

Spell work during this point usually focuses on positive energy, and the waxing crescent is ideal for attraction and protection magic. Potential spells here include protection, healing, wealth, success, friendship, luck, self-improvement, or inner beauty. You can accomplish much during this lunar phase, and it is a time for self-reflection and working toward your future goals and dreams. The waxing crescent comes about 3 to 7 days after the new moon, and its main theme is manifestation.

Waxing Crescent Spell Idea: you can try bath magic in this part of the cycle. You could use elements you already have, like water and salt, which are cleansing components that can be used in this ritual. So, run a bath and add bath or sea salts, whichever is at your disposal. You could also light candles to set the mood and prepare the environment. After that, the ritual is as simple as taking a bath. While doing it, imagine all your intentions and goals manifesting before you visualize them. Also think about anything that might be holding you back and let those obstacles flow down the drain as you cleanse yourself.

First Quarter

This next phase happens when you see only half the moon illuminated. It is called the first quarter because, at this point, a quarter of the lunar cycle is complete. Depending on the world location, people might see distinct halves of the moon illuminated so you might encounter the right half, and someone else in another country might see the left half. This is a critical phase of the cycle, and much happens within it.

In the first quarter, it is time to face the obstacles and challenges in your path. While the waxing crescent was about self-reflection and pouring your heart out, the first quarter is more about attracting things to you. Focus on the elements that matter in this phase and on reaching your goals. The full moon approaches, and you have to be prepared. The first quarter is also when you make changes to your plan and work around any challenges you might face.

You need to use the first quarter phase to attract the points you want in life like friends, money, and love using spells. Other spells that work during this phase are mostly creative magic, including divination, growth, motivation, and strength. This phase's theme is luck, and it comes about 7 to 10 and a half days after the new moon.

First Quarter Ritual Idea: since the first quarter is the time to review your progress and face your journey's challenges, you can do a sacred water ritual here. To make sacred moon water, you need a glass of spring water, natural salt, a burned piece of incense. Add the salt and the incense to the water after blowing it out. Make two even glasses of sacred water, place them on your altar, and start the ritual. Meditate and review your intentions to see where your journey has taken you so far.

Waxing Gibbous

This covers the time between the first quarter and the full moon. The word waxing implies that the moon is growing in size, which it is, while gibbous is to signify its shape, and that translates waxing gibbous to "growing shape". The moon's illumination keeps growing bigger during this phase of the lunar cycle until it is illuminated, which marks the start of the next phase.

Things should come together, and you should feel more energetic and chase after your dreams and desires. The moon's energy will guide you here, and you will see your hopes and aspirations come to fruition. You need to believe that things are working for you and good works are coming your way. Yet, this phase is also one of patience. Things will take shape, but you must not rush the outcome. Instead, focus on tying up loose ends and developing, so you can achieve optimal results.

Spell wise; the waxing gibbous is ideal for constructive magic that can nurture and develop that for which you have been working. You might feel exhausted by this point and low on energy, but you can harness the moon's power to boost your power and confidence. You can do health, success, and motivation spells in this stage, and growth magic. The best time to work on spells in this stage is between the hours 10 and 11 at night, when you will have the most assistance from divine deities. You can expect to see a waxing gibbous 10 to 14 days after the new moon.

Waxing Gibbous Ritual Idea: as we mentioned, this is the last phase before the full moon, so it is time to revisit your intentions. Read them out loud to the moon goddess and reaffirm them. You have already planted the seeds, and it is time to check any alignments taking place for your plan to work. This spell or ritual can help you see signs from the universe you are on the right path. You need to blend (clockwise) frankincense, 1-star anise, and two pinches of dried rosemary with a mortar and pestle. When the ingredients are a fine powder, ask the deities to guide you and the universe to give you clear and loud signs to influence you on your journey.

Full Moon

This phase is when the moon's face is entirely lit by the sun. A full moon happens when the sun and the moon are on opposing sides of the earth. Theoretically, the moon is fully illuminated by the sun lasts for a few moments, but we also say it is a new moon because it looks that way, although it really isn't.

At this phase, it is beaming with the most potent energies during the lunar cycle, and it is the time to attract all good things to you. It is also time to heal from past emotional pains. For many witches, the full moon is a point where most magic can be performed, whether it is constructive or destructive. You could banish unwanted energies and influences from your life in this phase, perform divination magic, and create protection spells.

You must prioritize during this crucial time. The moon's energies are peaking, and you cannot waste such intensity on minor spells or unimportant quests. You should focus on your most important goals and dreams and how to achieve them. So, use the full moon's strength for the things that matter in your life. Everything should work out in this phase, after the preparations and effort during the earlier cycles. During a full moon, you can celebrate success after finding love or getting the job you wanted.

Yet, it might not go your way. Regardless of how it turns out, you need to accept it as what is and move on.

Remember that the full moon guides you in this phase, so your intuition is sharper than other times during the lunar cycle. So, be mindful of your thoughts and dreams and focus on the path you want to take because a higher power is guiding you. You can perform love and healing magic during a full moon, and divination, banishing, dreams, and spirituality spells. This phase's theme is power because the forces at work here are heightened compared to the other phases.

Full Moon Ritual Idea: this is the best time for divination and readings, as see the fruits of your labors when it is a full moon. It is also an ideal time for communicating with spirits and deities since the moon's power heightens your senses. This is why you feel energetic when it is a full moon, and you don't need as much sleep. Consider what you're willing to receive. You can sit with a view of the full moon and start the ritual. Focus your whole mind and soul on the moon, and keep staring at it until you two become one. In this deep meditative state, concentrate on your intentions and on receiving guidance from the Goddess. Did you get what you were hoping for? Then be thankful. If not, also be grateful and think about what you might change. After you're done, you need to ground yourself; eating something heavy helps here.

Waning Gibbous

Unlike waxing, meaning growing, waning means decreasing. So, the shape of the moon is declining here, and the illumination is receding. This stage lasts until the moon becomes half illuminated. The moon's energies repel rather than attract, which makes this the perfect chance to work on banishing spells and others to remove things from your life with a negative influence. You could also do spells to end toxic relationships or unsuccessful business endeavors. Spells aside, a waning gibbous moon is a good time to clean your living space, tend to the garden, and arrange your magical tools and objects.

Focus on the things stopping you from achieving your objectives in this phase and the elements that might be draining your energy. Take a moment to stop and think about your intentions and where your past actions have led you. Is this where you want to be? If not, what's blocking you from getting there? What has been the most significant influence over your life so far in your journey? These questions will help you think about the changes you need to make. The waning gibbous moon might also be a time to step backward and rest for a bit, as the moon's light is fading and surrendering to the dark of the night.

Cleansing magic is recommended here. You can do curse removals, cleansing spells, undo bindings, remove negativity, and spells to help you get the results you want. Know, though, that the spell work you do here need not be directed at a person or an object but could be applied to yourself. Instead of trying to banish a toxic lover from your life, try ridding yourself of your feelings for them or your insecurities and self-doubt. Empowering yourself might work much better than trying to influence others' actions, and it may also be more ethical. The best thing to do is to work on the negative auras surrounding you and your perceptions and doubts about your self-worth.

> **Waning Gibbous Ritual Idea:** You need to write down a list of all your fears, troubles, and insecurities so you can do this ritual. Some witches take this paper to a crossroads and get rid of it, but you don't have to do that. You could instead burn it and, with that, surrender to the moon's power as you banish and relinquish those doubts holding you from moving forward and getting what you need and deserve.

Third Quarter

The third-quarter moon is the exact antithesis of the first quarter. The opposite half of the moon is illuminated. This is also the stage that marks that the lunar cycle is three-quarters complete and is about to end. This is another opportune time to tackle the obstacles and challenges in your way. This moon phase can help you plow through your roadblocks helped by the moon's energy.

You can use the third quarter to quit that job you've been hating and wanting to leave for months, make final payments, fire staff, get rid of things you don't need, and return belongings to their rightful owners. You could also use this stage to get support from someone who could offer you guidance, such as a spiritual advisor or a financial planner. Listen to what they have to say and follow their advice, because it might just be the turning point you need. Don't give up and keep working on your goals and meditate to visualize your dreams coming to fruition.

The third quarter is a good time to practice divination to see what the following month has in store for you. As the moon fades, use magic to get clear of the obstacles you're facing and get rid of any negative influences. You can use spells to get rid of addictions, diseases, ailments, and any off-setting emotions that might be stopping you from getting the things you want. You could also engage in protection spells, break curses, and do health and dream magic in this phase.

> **Third Quarter Ritual Idea:** during this lunar stage, you can take a cleansing ritual bath while burning incense or herbs so you could cleanse what you need to let go of and release negative energies and banish harmful influences.

Waning Crescent

This is the final phase of the lunar cycle, and it starts when the sun illuminates less than half of the moon, which continues until the New Moon. You may also notice the effects of the earthshine during this phase. The waning crescent ends when the sun and the moon rise simultaneously, which marks the start of a new lunar cycle with a New Moon. Also known as the balsamic moon, the waning crescent is a time of restoration and healing. It is the time of the cycle when your energy subsides, shifting from dynamic to quiet and reflective. You can take this time to reflect on the previous cycle and what has transpired. Think about the things you learned and the changes that have happened. Take these lessons into consideration as you prepare for the next lunar cycle.

During this phase, banishing magic is considered at its most powerful. So, this is the time to get rid of anything troubling you, whether it is clutter around your home or heavy feelings weighing you down. It is also the time to end toxic relationships so you can focus on yourself and your recovery. Meditate and nurture yourself, and take this phase to recuperate, rest, and recharge your energy.

You can cast spells to get rid of negative influences in this phase, and spells to remove obstacles and bring you peace of mind. Use magic to tackle situations like divorce, separation, getting rid of stalkers, and protection. Remember this stage is about finding balance and slowing down to reflect on the past and resolve to help you move forward. Use this time to bid farewell to the things holding you back and no longer serving a meaningful purpose in your life.

Special Phases

As we mentioned earlier, there are special phases of the lunar cycle. Some of these don't happen every month, while others do. You must understand them and the magic you can practice.

Dark Moon: The dark moon happens on the eve of a new moon, and it is considered being the final day in a complete lunar cycle. The dark moon is often associated with darker aspects of the Moon Goddess pertaining to death and destruction, which is why it is ideal for destructive magic. You can do hexes, curses, banishing, divorce, separation, and protection spells. They are significantly more powerful if cast during a dark moon, amplified by this part of the lunar phase's power. It is better to channel these dark energies toward self-reflection and rebuilding. You can use this power to do healing and cleansing rituals. It's also a good time to meditate and perform divination rituals to try to get a glimpse into your future and see what awaits you.

Lunar Eclipse: Lunar eclipses don't come often, and it is a moon phase brimming with magical power, and you should never miss out on this opportunity. Lunar eclipses are often associated with change, and they symbolize major shifts in your life. Those changes can lead you closer to your goals and dreams. A lunar eclipse usually happens once every year when the sun and moon's powers connect and create harmony and balance between the female and male divine energies. This union between those two opposite powers can support you to do powerful magic that will allow you to achieve things you never thought were possible.

There are a few who believe that lunar eclipses are a manifestation of every moon phase's energies because the eclipse starts with a full moon that wanes until it goes dark. After that, the new moon's silver manifests, and the moon wanes to full again. So, it can be said that you have the energies of the different phases all at once. You can do all kinds of magic spells here, and they will be potent and powerful. Remember to keep timing in mind when performing rituals during a lunar eclipse because the phases will vary depending on where you're located. So, keep an eye on the local start and end times when you plan for this ritual. Spells you can do during a lunar eclipse include money, relationships, healing, wealth, protection, and divination.

Blue Moon: Whenever there are two full moons in a lunar cycle, the second one is called a Blue Moon. Some believe that the blue moon is much more powerful than a full moon, and it's used to do powerful and significant spells. A Blue Moon only happens every

2.5 years, and it usually falls on a different month every year. Exercise caution when practicing magic during this special moon phase because the outcome might be exponentially more effective than you predict.

Many witches believe that the Blue Moon is a time where the veil between our world and that of the spirits is very thin, which can facilitate any communication between both worlds. During this time, you will have heightened powers and clarity, and this is why it is ideal for divination. Your magic will be amplified, and your psychic skills will also most likely be at their peak. So, seize this rare opportunity to harness the moon's power and use it to your advantage. Spells and magic that happen during the Blue Moon often have long-term consequences, so always remember that and don't use a spell when you are not sure about the effects.

It is ideal to plant new seeds and ideas that could help you move forward toward your dreams because they will have long-term effects, and you will see significant changes in your life. Meditation is highly recommended during this moon phase, as is divination because of your heightened powers and abilities.

Chapter 3: Moon Spellcasting: Tools and Preparation

Spellcasting is an intricate process that requires an understanding of the world of magic, and more important, having the necessary tools to perform rituals and spells. For some, it can be an easy process, while for others, it's very complicated. In this chapter, we will cover the tools and items you will need to cast spells and how you should prepare. Once you grasp the basic objects you will need, and optional ones, spellcasting becomes more about the magic rather than scrambling to find the tools and ingredients. You need certain items you cannot perform your spells without, which we will explore during this chapter for moon spells. A witch will also need to prepare to perform these spells and ready her mind, body, and spirit to delve into the magic and spell casting, which we will also cover in this chapter.

Tools for Spell Casting

So, what is the point of these tools and items? Wiccans believe these tools are used in rituals to honor the deities and channel the moon's psychic energies to help perform a certain action. These are the most common tools that a witch needs to cast spells and perform rituals.

Altar

The first item we will talk about is a basic one that any witch needs to have. The altar is a sacred space in which you will store all your ritual tools and ingredients. More important, the altar is used as a workspace when you perform and make spells. Many people commonly use a table as an altar, but that might not be ideal if you want a mobile altar. Several witches use a portable case to use an altar, and they can store their tools and ingredients in something as simple as a drawer.

The importance of an altar extends beyond having a space to store your tools and perform the rituals. The altar is often used to connect with the deities who will guide you on your ritual, which is why altars have always been important in pagan rituals. People put so much emphasis on altars they have more than one at home, each for a certain ceremony or ritual.

There isn't a correct way to set up an altar; it's your magical space, and you can do with it what you will and set it up; however you please. Practitioners like to add decorative touches like a special scarf or cover for the altar. As for the altar's material, use wood, ceramic, or stone because these elements ground the energy, and you can also engrave any symbols or ritualistic inscriptions into them.

Altar Accessories

You don't just buy an altar and start performing rituals. You need to get the objects and accessories that are going to be using with the altar. This starts with candleholders for all the rituals in which you will light candles to set the environment and cast a spell. You will also need incense burners because many spells require burning incense. Crystals may be needed and vases for flowers. Some of these items aren't used for magic per se, but they give the magical items you do use their potency, and they also create a beautiful and sacred space to practice your rituals and cast your spells.

Athame and Other Blades

One of the essential tools for performing spells is a blade, commonly called an *athame* in witchcraft. It usually comes with a black handle and is made from pure metal; it is not supposed to be a knife to cut herbs or used as a regular knife, so it is not sharpened since it doesn't have practical uses. The athame is used to indicate directions, direct energy, and cut a way out of the circle safely without compromising your energy. It is believed this blade represents the masculine energy and the air element.

An athame might also be used as a wand. You use another blade to cut herbs, called a *boline,* which is shaped like a crescent moon and comes with a white handle. The boline is also used to inscribe candles. Sometimes, for more advanced witches, a sword is used to mark sacred circles of great significance and size. But usually only the high priestess of a coven may use it.

Burin

A burin is not exactly a blade; it's a small tool with a thin point used by witches to carve words and symbols into candles, wood, and other magical objects. You can make it out of whatever material you please, such as pins or nails or any other similar item.

Wands

A wand can be made out of any natural material, though it is most commonly made from wood, rock, or metal. It symbolizes the Air element, in some traditions, Fire, and it is often used to summon entities and invoke deities. A wand is also used to direct energy, bless something, and consecrate sacred spaces or magical items.

Broom or Besom

This is one of the more personal spell casting tools. You can have one custom made from the twigs of a tree of your choice or make it yourself. You don't use a broom or besom for sweeping and cleaning dirt; it is used to cleanse negative energies and remove bad influences, usually before spell work. To use a besom or broom, gently sweep the room in a clockwise direction, rid it of any negative energies, open the door, throw the energy outside, and close the door afterward. A lot of witches considered their brooms sacred, and many believe they should never touch the ground. Some use the broom or besom in seasonal fertility dances or with other traditions.

Bells and Rattles

In many ancient civilizations, hundreds of years ago, they used bells to ward off evil and dark spirits. The vibrations coming from a bell were also believed to be the source of great power. Bells were used to summon spirits, not just banish them. You ring a bell in the corner of a room to get rid of dark energies and evil presence. You can also use rattles and singing bowls to bring peace and harmony to a sacred space or cleanse a magic ritual.

Grimoire

A book of shadows or a grimoire is another important tool in a witch's arsenal. It is a notebook where you journal and document your magical practices and spell work. Each witch writes their grimoire, and it usually chronicles everything they've learned on their journey, including spells, rituals, invocations, moon charts, and a list of deities and pantheons. While the book of shadows is a highly personal tool that witches keep private and secure, it can sometimes be passed from one to the other, though it usually remains within the family.

Candles

Candles are an indispensable part of witchcraft, and witches must always have access to them. Fortunately, the candles are cheap and can easily be found anywhere. They also attract little attention, which makes it easy for witches to practice their magic. There are even dedicated branches of magic for candles and the spells you can do with them. Candles can summon deities, for manifestation, and several other spells. They represent the element of Fire in spells and rituals, and they often symbolize the God and the Goddess in Wicca. Another candle usage is in spell work, where they are utilized to absorb the witch's energy and then release it as the candle burns.

Chalice

A chalice or a goblet is not necessarily a tool for spell making, but many witches believe that it is a symbol of the Goddess or her womb. It is also symbolic of the element of Water. There are certain similarities between the chalice and the Holy Grail, though, in witchcraft, its symbolism is much different. It does not represent the blood of Christ but rather the womb of the Goddess. It can be filled with wine or water and passed around a group of witches practicing magic, or it could be wine offered to the Goddess.

Cauldron

Despite its somewhat comic use in films and cartoons, a cauldron is an essential tool for witchcraft and spell making. It's used to burn incense and herbs, brew potions, perform water scrying to enhance visions and look into other realms, and make offerings. This three-legged vessel is usually made from cast iron.

The cauldron can also hold large pillar candles. Many modern cauldrons are portable and can easily be moved around.

Compass

Acknowledging the four cardinal directions is often a prerequisite for many spells and rituals. Not every witch has an excellent sense of direction, which is why a compass sometimes proves to be integral during spell work. It will help you orient yourself in the right direction so you can harness the right energies and align yourself properly.

Crystals

Crystals are another essential item for making spells and performing magic. They hold within them the earth's energy, each with a unique frequency that allows it to vibrate at a different level. Crystals have varying purposes, and you will need to use the ones suited for the spell you are making. Crystals are used for healing, while others are used for manifestation. Generally, crystals are also great for meditation. Remember to choose one depending on your intentions for the spell work. You should regularly clean your crystals, and more importantly, recharge them either during a full moon or by burying them in the earth while you sleep at night.

Clothes

There isn't a uniform dress code for doing magic, but witches have personal preferences with their attire when performing spells or rituals. Many believe that colors can affect the flow of energies and how they move, which is why many witches wear black during rituals to keep from scattering any energy or causing distraction. You could also wear ritual clothes like a cloak, robe, or mask so you can achieve the right mindset to perform the magic you need.

Jewelry is common during rituals and spell casting, especially for Wiccans. Many witches and practitioners wear jewelry displaying pentacles or other pagan and religious symbols during rituals and spell casting, and they can also be worn during everyday life. In several forms of Wicca, people wear a necklace with a circle to signify the circle of rebirth.

Divination Tools

Divination is one of the essential practices for witches, and you will need certain tools to practice divination. Start with a crystal ball, oracle cards, tarot cards, scrying mirrors, and pendulums because each of these will have a very important use when performing divination. You will use these items to look into the future, receive messages and information from deities and mystical powers, confirm your intuition about something, and communicate with your guides on a psychic level. You won't necessarily use those tools; most witches don't; they just use one or two. You just need to find certain divination tools you can master and keep practicing until you perfect your gift with those tools.

Spear

While a spear is not an essential item for spell casting, it is still one of the more popular witchcraft tools for many Wiccans. It is believed to represent the Horned God in rituals that invoke him. This is why several traditional Wiccan rituals require this spear.

Herbs

We've mentioned herbs several times already, and that is because they play a very important role in spell casting. Herbs hold the energy of the earth, each with its unique signature and importance. Herbs can be used in many spells, and they can also be used as incense, in smudging, and for kitchen witchery, and in baths and other self-care rituals. It's always a good idea to have a mortar and pestle if you are going to be working with herbs because they will help you crush the herbs and mix them into powders.

Pen and Paper

You will notice that several spells require the witch to write something down, such as your dreams, desires, or emotions you want to get rid of. This is why you must always have a pen and paper nearby for such cases. You will burn papers if you're doing certain spells, and for others, you will do nothing with the paper. So, be mindful of the paper you get for your spells. Some kinds burn faster than others, while other types shouldn't even be burned. As for pens, you should have a few on hand and include various colors because color magic demands so. Witches recommend charging your paper or pen by waving them through the smoke of the incense, preferably during phases where the energy coming from the moon is at its peak.

Incense

We also mentioned incense several times since it is another basic spell-making item you always need. Incense is a powerful tool that can focus your energies and intentions for manifestation. You can also meditate with incense since it helps channel your energy and focus your thoughts and feelings. Incense is also crucial for cleansing rituals and blessings of a space. You can use it to purify yourself and other members in a magic circle. Incense often comes in different forms and smells. It can be sold as cones or sticks, and the varying fragrances might serve different spells or rituals.

Pentacle

Many people confuse pentagrams and pentacles, and the difference can be confusing. The pentagram is a five-pointed star, and the pentacle is the same, but the star is enclosed in a circle. Other symbols might be engraved on the pentacle, but the pentagram is the one most commonly used. It is a protective amulet often made from wood, but it can also be made from wax, metal, or clay. Some witches believe the pentacle represents the Earth element, and it is used on altars for different purposes like blessing items and tools. It is also used to charge objects, like crystals or chalices.

Offering Bowl

Some witches follow a religious path, and they offer sacrifices or offerings to their deities. If you're going to do that, you will need an offering bowl in which to place those offerings to the Gods and Goddesses.

Lunar Calendar

Finally, any witch who wants to cast spells during the moon phases must have a lunar calendar, also known as an almanac, with the detailed phases of the moon. This will help you prepare the spells and rituals you want to perform throughout the month because, as we mentioned earlier, you should not cast spells haphazardly. Each spell needs to be cast at exactly the right time, so you get the desired result.

Preparing for the Spells

The most powerful magical tool is you. Spells are about your energy, belief, and willpower. This is why you have to prepare yourself spiritually and mentally for spell casting, so you achieve the desired outcome. Here is what you can do.

1. Preparations

Timing: You can't just wake up from your afternoon nap and start concocting spells. You need to prepare first, and you have to be in a certain state of mind. The first thing you need to do is select an appropriate time for the spell. Go through your lunar calendar and select the best time of night to cast your spell, when the moon's powers are at its peak and ready to be harnessed. The more accurate your timing, the more potent your spell will be.

Location: The second thing you need to think about is the location you will prepare your spell. Sometimes, the success of the ritual will depend on the location. You have to find a place where you can be undisturbed so you can focus and channel your energy, somewhere calming. It is also preferred that rituals and spells are done outdoors where the setting is natural and near the earth. Sometimes it might not be easy to find an outdoor location. If so, try to get as close to nature as you can. Finally, make sure you have enough space for your ritual.

Review the Spell: The first time you read a spell should not be the first time you perform it. Take the time to review the spell and familiarize yourself with it. Don't memorize it, but it should come to you naturally and flow smoothly. You do not want to become flustered or forgetful while crafting the spell or ritual because this will affect the outcome.

Prepare the Tools: After reviewing the spell and understanding the tools, you'll need, collect them, and prepare them for the ritual. Don't wait until the last moment because you don't want to waste your window when it comes to lunar alignment. Prepare the tools and space for the ritual beforehand and make sure everything you will need is within reach.

2. Self-Care

You are the most important magical tool, and you need to prepare yourself for whatever rituals or spells you will engage in. Before casting spells, remember to eat light meals and snacks in the hours before. You don't want food to weigh you down or make you feel sleepy. You need to be centered and focused so you can get the best results from your magic and spells.

Also, meditate. This will help clear your mind and put you in the right mindset to practice magic. Take the time to achieve this by meditating and centering yourself. Dampen the lights, put on soothing music, light candles, and close your eyes. Focus on ridding yourself of any negative energies and find your center. Take your time with this because meditating can be the difference between a successful ritual and a failed one.

You could also try a cleansing ritual to purify yourself. Revert to the cleansing ritual we mentioned earlier in the book and perform it before casting spells. Fill a bath with water and essential oils and natural salts. They will help purify you and cleanse you of negative energies.

3. Cleansing the Space

Before you cast spells, cleanse the magical space you'll be working in. This will help get rid of any negative energies and unwanted frequencies. You can use natural earth elements to help you with the cleanse. Find sea salt, rock salt, and a few fabric bags. Mix the salts in the bags and place them in the four corners of the room. Say out loud that you are cleansing this space of any negative energies and forces. You need to visualize that happening, not just say it. Picture the negative energies and frequencies, leaving your magical space.

You can burn incense to further purify the location. Use a smudge stick like cedar or Sweetgrass. You just light the stick until it burns and then blow on it. The smoke will keep coming, and you can use it to smudge the entire space and cleanse it all--move in a clockwise direction with the stick. Like with the previous ritual, visualize and imagine the negative energies escaping your magical space.

4. State of Mind

Your state of mind makes a difference in the ritual and how things will turn out. You need to be in a conducive mindset because it will help you reach your goals. Mental discipline is key here, and meditation can help you reach that level where you can be so focused on your goals and visions that all else disappears. You need to keep a positive mindset in the days and hours leading up to your spell casting. You already know the time when you will cast your spells, and, until that day comes, you need to immerse yourself in positive thoughts.

Avoid worrying about your spells and rituals' success because this is the easiest way for them not to work. During the spell, you need to practice a heightened state of awareness; your mind needs to be conducive for magic and at peak energy so you can attain the required results. You need to access your subconscious while remaining conscious and focused on the moment. It might sound complicated, but with enough training and discipline, you will get there.

Your positive thoughts need to continue even after the spell is cast. If you let your mind wander to negativity or self-doubt, you could ruin everything for which you have worked. The best thing you can do is to not think about a spell you've performed; if you do, try to keep positive thoughts. As a distraction, you can prepare for your next spell.

Section 2: Practical Moon Spells

Chapter 4: Love Spells

By now, you will understand the different lunar phases and their significance, the moon and the energy and power you can harness through it, and how the different phases can be utilized to your advantage if you make the right spell at the right time. We then explored the tools you can use to cast spells and practice magic. Now it is time to get into practicalities and how to cast such spells.

The first spells we will be exploring are love spells. From Goddesses to witches, love spells have been around for millennia, used to draw someone's love and attention or get rid of it. A love spell is simply an enchantment you cast during the proper lunar phase so you can change your fortunes when it comes to love. No matter the problems you're facing romantically, this spell can help you. A love spell could help you start or resume a relationship with someone who you have been dreaming about for months. It could also help you get over a breakup or move on from a past relationship.

A love spell can be cast to attract a new lover or make someone fall in love with you, though you need to be careful with the latter. A love spell can also strengthen the bond of love you have with your partner and help progress the relationship to the next level--those who want to get married but feel that their partners have cold feet, take note.

With love, spells, potency, and efficiency make a lot of difference. Unless the spell is cast perfectly, you will not get the results you want. If you're doing it wrong, it doesn't matter if you cast the spell 20 times; it still doesn't work. So, follow the instructions presented to get the results you want every time you cast a love spell.

Tips

For love spells to work, you must focus on your intention before you do anything. You can't just utter the words and hope for the best; you need to believe this will work, and you need to fully know the consequences and outcomes of your actions because this is how they can come to be. You can't be sleepy, distracted, or under the influence while performing a love spell, or any other spell. You need to have your wits about you, and you must know your senses. Your intentions need to be genuine and of good nature. You are trying to change your future, and you cannot try such a feat on a whim.

It's important that you also determine the desired outcome of the love spell before you cast it. There is no such thing as casting a general love spell and hoping good things will come to fruition in your life; your goals need to be focused and clear so you can reach them. The best advice with a love spell is to focus on your own emotions and feelings rather than trying to influence other people's feelings because you would likely not want the same done to you, but if you are comfortable influencing others, then you can move forward and work on the love spell as intended.

Another thing to remember with love spells is your feelings. You can't have two lovers in mind when you're casting this spell; you have to be certain of your feelings. Your feelings cannot fluctuate, or else you risk the spell not working. There has to be certainty and conviction in every step you take, or else things might not go your way.

One final thing to always remember with love spells specifically is to manage your expectations. You must believe in your love spells' outcome, but that does not mean you shouldn't have realistic expectations. The spell won't drop prince charming in your lap the next day, nor will it have Hollywood's most eligible bachelor fall in love with you. If the spell aims to make someone fall in love with you, you need a preexisting relationship with that person and some prior connection, or it won't make sense for the spell to work. The goal of the spell, would be trying to bring forth more abundance and love into your existing relationship rather than trying to change someone's feelings or perceptions so they will notice you.

Lunar Phase

Spells cannot be cast randomly; they need to be cast at specific times following the lunar phases so you can get the desired outcome. The best time to cast a love spell is during a Full Moon, where the moon's energy is at its peak, and you can harness and channel those energies, but this does not mean you cannot cast a love spell at other times during the lunar cycle, though the nature of those spells will vary. To attract new love, you should cast a love spell during the Waxing Moon phase. To end a relationship and get rid of your feelings for someone, then your spell should be cast during the Waning Moon phase. The New Moon is also a great time to cast spells to manifest love and other positive things you want in your life.

Now that you understand when you can cast your love spells, it is time to learn how. Again, remember to focus on your intentions and believe in the positive outcome of your magic. Do that, and those spells will change the course of your future. Before you work on your love magic, remember to cleanse yourself and your magic space of any negative energy and vibrations. This is not an optional step because you need your space to be clear of any hate or other negative emotions so you can start the rituals with a pure soul and in a cleansed space.

Spell 1: Facilitating Love

The first love spell we will discuss is a New Moon ritual to manifest love and abundance in your life. If you have an existing relationship with a person and want to bring forth more abundance and love in that relationship, this is the spell to cast. This ritual starts by creating a sacred space that is calm and relaxing, so you need to declutter and cleanse the space first. The tools you will need are a pen or pencil and paper. Light a candle at your altar and smudge the place with sage or use essential oils. Then you need to think about the relationship that you'd like to manifest in your life. Think about the qualities and how you want your partner to be, and write those things down along with your intentions.

Then, place a rose quartz crystal on the paper because that is a powerful magical tool for manifesting and attracting love, and it also promotes self-love, which you need for this ritual to work. Now that you have written your intentions and goals, it is time to meditate on them. Close your eyes to the relaxing effects of the candle and think about and visualizing your intentions. The more you believe in them, the better your chances will be of them manifesting and coming to fruition.

Spell 2: Attracting Love

This ritual is like its predecessor, with minor differences that will help you attract new love. This spell is the best cast during the waxing moon phase, which is the perfect time to attract new things to your life and draw more love and affection that will change your life for the better. You will need a piece of paper and a pen with red ink. You will also need a candle, but it has to be a red one.

Start by lighting the candle and slowly delve into a deep meditative state, focusing on the candle's smoke. Clear your mind of negative thoughts and focus on what you want to attract during this lunar cycle. Then, write down on the piece of paper what you want to happen in your romantic life and what you want to attract. The candle wax would already be dripping at this point; let it drip onto the piece of paper after you have written the things you want to attract romantically. The last thing you need to do is to bind the spell, and you can do that by calling on the Goddess - usually Venus for this spell - and asking her to lead someone into your life because you deeply love them and are attracted to them.

After you're done with the spell, sit down and meditate for a while and keep visualizing this person entering your life. Focus on your intentions and believe that good things are coming your way.

Spell 3: New Romance

There is always hope for a new romance, especially with this particular spell. Have a coworker that does not think about you, romantically? This ritual can help change that. You will need a photograph of the person you want to fall in love with you. You will also need blue and red candles and incense, preferably rosewood. This spell is the best cast during a New Moon.

The ritual starts with lighting the candles, blue for luck, and red for love. Light the rosewood incense so you could get into the right mindset and relax before casting your love spell. After relaxing and getting into the right frame of mind, face the picture of your desired lover and kneel before them. Then, invoke the Goddess and express your intent of gaining attention and love from this person. Close your eyes, focus on your intentions coming true and meditate for a while in the same position. Don't think about anything else at that point but your goal and this person falling for you.

Spell 4: Finding the Perfect Partner

This spell utilizes rose petal magic, which can be very potent if done right. It is an easy spell, though you might meet challenges trying to find the right moment to cast it. You will need rose petals to perform this ritual and a body of water like a river or the ocean. This spell is the best cast during the Waxing Moon or a Full Moon, so you can harness the moon's energy and channel it to attract the perfect partner.

The first thing you need to do is think about if that partner is perfect for you. What qualities do you want them to have? Think long about that and visualize the person with all those qualities. Next, throw your rose petals into the moving body of water, asking your guides or deities to bring you true love, as those petals are moving out to the seas or open waters. Repeat this ritual twice, all while visualizing your ideal partner and thinking about your intent.

After casting these love spells, you mustn't obsess with the outcome. This can form negative energies that could jeopardize the outcome of your ritual. Obsessing is never a good idea, and the same goes for when you're practicing magic. A love spell can work if you stay patient and think positively. So, give the spell time to work without losing your patience and trying to rush the results. Have faith and trust that good things are coming your way.

Chapter 5: Fertility Spells

The association between the moon and fertility has been an everlasting one throughout countless civilization. Beyond spiritual beliefs, several studies have also found that the female menstrual cycle is also linked to the different moon phases, which does not come as a surprise considering how the moon is the representation of the female deity. Some of the most important spells and rituals you can practice during the lunar cycle are associated with fertility.

Witches practice fertility spells during the moon phases for different reasons. Some seek to enhance their fertility and increase their chances of getting pregnant, others try to make sure that their newborn is healthy and well, and some try to secure safe delivery. Fertility spells are not just associated with childbirth. Fertility can also mean abundance and bringing more good and wealth into your life. This section will explore spells that you can practice promoting fertility and abundance in your life using magic and sacred rituals.

Fertility Ritual

The first ceremony we will be talking about is a moon fertility ritual. It is best done during the waxing to full moon phases, though you have to sync those with your own body as a female if you are trying to increase your fertility and get pregnant. If so, then this spell is the best cast two weeks after your cycle begins. If this spell is cast to increase a man's fertility, then the spell's timing does not matter as much. As for the time of day to cast this spell, it is the best cast during the early evening hours when you are at your most creative and focused.

Tools: You will need lots of incense for this moon fertility ritual. Get sandalwood incense since it is said to promote mental fertility, and peach incense because it promotes physical fertility and abundance. Don't forget to source an incense burner naturally so you can move around freely with the smoke if you need it.

Deities: This will depend on your set of beliefs and the deities in which you believe, but for Wiccans, there are particular deities you can invoke for this fertility ritual, including Ishtar, Freyr, Brigid, and obviously Diana.

To prepare for this ritual, cast a magical circle. As always, cleanse the magical space and the circle before you begin the ritual. You need to get into the right mindset before starting, so also meditate if that helps you relax. Cleanse your mind of any negative thoughts and feelings. Visualize your negative vibrations dissipating slowly from your body and focus on your intentions. Then, light the incense and state your purpose for this ritual. Invoke the deities that guide you and declare out loud to them your goal and what you want to carry out through this ritual.

As the incense burns, imagine its smoke filling you and touching you, especially the parts of you that you want to be fertile. This ritual dictates you implore each of the four directions, starting with the east. Reach out to the four elementals and implore them to help make you fertile and fill your life with joy. Then, after you've implored the four elements in the four directions, lie down on the floor facing north, stretching your arms and legs. Call out to the deities you invoked here and ask them to bless your loins and make you fertile. Relax and feel the moon's energy wash over you to fill your body with power and fertility.

Kneel before your altar and bless the food you have there. You should have a salad with cucumber and carrots, and olive oil and garlic dressing, a banana, and flavored tea. This food should be consumed after the ritual not to fill you up, but to give you energy. Imagine the food you're consuming, filling the infertile parts of you with energy, and changing that part to be fertile as you slowly eat.

To conclude this ritual, ground yourself and meditate. Find your center and close your circle as you slowly focus on your intents and visualize yourself becoming fertile. If this spell's purpose is to make you fertile and have kids, engage in sexual activity within a day of finishing the spell so you can see its effect coming to fruition. Remember to have faith and believe this spell will work. Hopefully, you will soon become fertile, and your blessed loins will bear a child.

Fertility Spell

This next spell is a very easy one to cast because its ingredients and concept are simple. As always, the most important part of this spell is you. The energy you bring into this spell will determine whether it will work, so be mindful of the vibrations you bring and watch your feelings and intent. This Wiccan fertility spell requires a pen, blossom powder, jasmine spiritual oil, Adam and Eve spiritual oil, and a red female figure candle, plus a plate.

Start by writing your name on the bottom of the female figure candle. After you've done that, place the candle on the plate and then add the jasmine and Adam and Eve spiritual oils and the blossom powder to cover the candle. With the mixture covering the body, rub it with your fingers over the female figure's stomach. Then, stand the candle up on the plate and light it.

You can invoke your deities at this point and ask them to bless your loins with fertility so you can have kids. Close your eyes and meditate, visualizing this spell working and your infertile body changing to become fertile. You must put positive energy into this spell, or else it would not work. Do not obsess over the spell's outcome, but believe that it will work, and you will find fertility and abundance. Don't dwell on negative thoughts, or else you might jeopardize the success of the fertility spell.

Full Moon Spell

This is a full moon fertility spell you can do to promote fertility and ask the Goddess to help you bear a child. It needs to be performed on a full moon, as we've mentioned, preferably on a Monday around 7 pm or 7:30 pm. This spell takes a few more steps than the previous one, and you will need more ingredients, but don't let that deter you. Just focus on finding each ingredient, and then we'll walk you through how you can use them.

Tools/Ingredients: You will need a pen or pencil and paper, three taper candles (pink, blue, and green), cinnamon oil, sandalwood incense, a bowl of soil, a small box or jar, and a baby blanket--if you already have a baby, you could use their blanket for this spell, which would make it more potent and efficient.

Before you cast the spell, you need to first cleanse yourself. Take a ritual bath with natural oils, especially cinnamon oil. This will help rid you of any lingering negative energies and cleanse your body. After you're done, prepare all your tools and ingredients and start your spell.

Cast a magical circle and light the incense. Invoke the deities that guide you or the Goddess. You must take your time with this step because these deities will come to join your circle and guide you on this journey. They will hear your prayers and help you reach your goals. Take the fresh soil you've gathered and sprinkled it around your circle, honoring the Goddess and asking her to provide you with fertility. After that, cover your altar with the baby blanket and pray to the gods and goddesses, declaring this is the blanket with which you will cover your little one.

Then, you need to take the three candles and place them next to one another, with the green one at the center, blue to its left, and pink to its right. As you do this, keep praying to the deities and declare these are the candles that will light your womb. Next, take the green candle, lather it with cinnamon oil, and picture your child. You need to see them in your mind's eye. Picture yourself pregnant with them and then giving birth. Visualize holding the fruit of your loins in your arms and hold on to that mental image. Put the green candle back in the center of the table.

Light the other two candles and use them to light the green candle. As you do so, declare your intent to the Gods and Goddesses. Pray to them and ask them to give you a boy or a girl, pink for girls and blue for boys. After you finish chanting and praying to the deities, take the pen and paper and write down the names you want for a boy and a girl. Put both papers inside the box or jar you've prepared earlier and placed it in front of the green candle. Then let the candle burn down until it extinguishes itself and then place the box somewhere safe. Finally, engage in a sexual relationship with your partner and wait for the spell to work.

As with previous spells, remember not to dwell or obsess about the success of your fertility spell. Place your faith in the spell and let it disappear from your mind. If you can't help thinking about it, make sure your thoughts are positive. Let go of negative thoughts or fears.

Safe Childbirth Spell

Another very important spell that witches cast for fertility concerns the newborn's health and well-being. No one has full control over such matters, and unfortunately, it happens often that a newborn is in poor health and needs help that others cannot give. This is why safe childbirth spells are common, and they can help you to increase the chance that your child is born in good health.

To do this spell, you won't need many items. You need a green candle with a pine scent and an apple. Remember this spell is done after conceiving, and you do it if you are concerned that your child might be born with an inherent problem or in bad health. Take one half of the apple and rub it over your belly and then close your eyes and meditate. Visualize the sickness and bad health being drawn out of your womb and the child growing within it like poison from a wound. After you've done so, take that bad half of the apple and bury it in the earth far away from your child's room.

Eat the other half of the apple and picture your child being born and living a healthy and happy life. You can light the pine-scented candle as you eat the apple; they have healing effects, and pine is linked to fertility and Mother Earth.

Wash up and cleanse yourself. If a tree grows from the buried apple remains, then your child will grow strong and will connect to the earth. Again, the most important part of this spell is your energy and ability to visualize your child living a happy and healthy life, free of disease and suffering. So, focus on your intent and keep a positive mindset throughout this entire spell.

Chapter 6: Money and Career Spells

Money and career spells are very important for witches who want to find wealth and satisfaction in their lives. These spells are great for those who would like a break in their careers or the chance to advance and grow professionally. The spells that we will discuss in this chapter can help you find wealth and attract money and the career opportunities you have been waiting for all your life. If you want a raise or a promotion in your current job, these spells could also help.

You might think casting a spell to get money is hard but thinking so is what makes it hard. You need to believe this will work. Channeling the flow of money into your life is just channeling certain energy, and once you connect to your inner power and tap into the moon's energy, there is no energy flow out there that you cannot control. So, work on your belief and visualizing the money you need for that new house or car.

Full Moon Money Spell

The full moon is the time when the moon's power is at its peak, and you can harness that power to your advantage to channel money into your life. There are other times when you can cast money spells, but we will be talking about a full moon money spell for this first ritual. Wait for this part of the lunar cycle to come by so you can get the most from the spell, amplifying its effects. This spell is naturally cast overnight so you can harness the moon's energy. It is practiced best if you can see the direct moonlight coming through your window. It can work if it is shrouded in clouds, but try to wait until the light is unveiled for most potency.

The tools you need for this spell might sound complicated, but the spell is a lot easier than it sounds. You will first need a mirror and don't worry about mirrors being bad luck. They are ordinary objects that can be charged with certain energies. More important, they can help you amplify the moon's energy to make your spell even more powerful. Find a small round mirror, though any shape will work. You will then need a permanent marker and cinnamon oil (you can use ground cinnamon also for this spell). You need three coins; they should be gold coins, but other types might work. The last thing you need for this spell to work is a green pouch that is spacious enough to accommodate the coins and the mirror.

To start this spell, you need to find a clear view of the full moon. If you have a small private garden, that will be ideal, but if you can be bathed in the moon's glow, the spell will be potent. Gather all your ingredients and sit facing the moon. Close your eyes, calm your mind, and relax. Try to get into a meditative state to clear your thoughts. If you are indoors, open the window to get air. Put the mirror on a surface where the moonlight can hit it.

With the marker, draw the symbols of wealth and prosperity on the mirror's center—there are several Wiccan symbols you can use here, like the key and the number 3. Then, take the cinnamon oil or powder and dip your finger in it and then draw a circle around the symbol of prosperity you have drawn. Don't drown the mirror in oil or powder; use just enough to draw a circle. The next step is to put the three coins you've prepared evenly on the circle of cinnamon oil or powder, marking the symbol of prosperity. Close your eyes again and delve into a meditative state as the moon charges your tools with its power. Focus on your intents and be very specific here.

Focus exactly on the things you want with as much specificity as possible, whether it is determining the amount of money you need or the type of promotion. Immerse yourself in the feelings you will have when you receive that money and visualize it happening. In this immersive state, imagine the moon's light and power washing over you, and then channel that energy and everything you want into the mirror. Open your eyes, invoke the deities, declare your intents, and ask them to guide you to get the money you need.

Finally, take the coins and drop them consecutively into the green pouch, and then slowly put the mirror on top of the coins. Close the pouch and keep it somewhere safe where you can look at it whenever you want until your desires manifest. You can repeat this ritual on the next full moon using the same ingredients, but use fresh cinnamon the second time around.

Spell to Get a Job

There comes a point in every person's professional life when they want a job. This can come early on or later in your career, but it always comes, and you may need a little help to make things go your way. This spell should only be performed after you've submitted your resume or applied for the job. It can help you get the job that your heart desires, but you need to be specific with this spell to get the desired results. As always, believing this spell will work goes a long way toward it working.

They need a sharp tool, like a knife or a pin, green and red candles, and milk. This Wiccan spell starts with writing the company's name you want to work for on the large green candle. Then, on the red candle, carve *Tiwaz*, also known as the victory rune, which is like an arrow facing upward, besides your full name.

This spell should take place on a Thursday. Burn both candles on a Thursday evening for half an hour, and then snuff them out, but don't blow the candles out. Leave a bowl of milk overnight, outside your house, as an offering to the Gods and Goddesses. Repeat this ritual every Thursday at the same hour, but let the candles burn for 15 minutes. Repeat until the candles burn out, or the job is yours.

New Moon Promotion Spells

A person often is passed over for promotions they deserve, which isn't fair but happens, nonetheless. Climbing up the corporate ladder is not as easy as you might think, and you may need magical help. This spell is used to help you do just that, and it can help you get that elusive promotion.

This is a new moon spell, so you have to wait until a new lunar cycle casts it, which makes sense considering that you are looking for a new beginning, which is what this lunar phase is associated with. Prepare your altar for this magical ritual and cleanse your space of any negative energies. Find gold glitter and place it in a jar on your altar as you picture yourself getting the promotion. Clear your mind and focus only on climbing up the corporate ladder and achieving your professional goals.

After that, find the stairs and climb those stairs with the jar held in your hand. You need to have faith and confidence while you are climbing those stairs because this step represents you climbing the corporate ladder and attaining your professional goals. While climbing the stairs, declare your intentions, and invoke the deities to guide you until you get that promotion you are after. After reaching the top of the stairs, put down the jar of gold and meditate. Visualize yourself getting the job and working on it until you achieve success and prosperity.

New Moon Money Ritual

This is a ritual to attract money, and it needs to be done at the start of a new lunar cycle. Wait for the new moon and prepare the items you need for this ritual to work. It is simple, and all you will need is three green candles. The ritual starts by lighting those three candles as you dive into a contemplative mood and meditate. Focus on wealth and the amount of money you want to attract to your life.

Then, invoke the deities or your guides and pray to them. Pray to them and ask them to fill your life with money and abundance, all while focusing clearly on your intents and the money you want to invite to your life. Remember to always focus on a specific amount, don't be vague. Keep burning those candles every day while declaring and renewing your intents until the money manifests. Repeat the prayers every time you light the candles and do this until the candles are gone or until the money manifests.

Ritual for Performance Reviews

Everybody dreads a performance review. It feels like your work is under the microscope, and the review might also decide whether you qualify for a raise which makes it a very important step to a healthy career. You can cast this spell to get the most out of your performance review you often dread. This spell is the best cast a day before the time of the review.

This ritual starts with you putting on the exact clothes you will be wearing for the performance review. Ground yourself and calm your mind while sitting in a chair. Put meditative music on in the background. Close your eyes and reflect on your journey since you got the job or since the last review. Think about your accomplishments and the things you want to mention to prompt your superiors to give you a raise or a promotion. Write those reasons and accomplishments down on a piece of paper. Then, place the paper in your pocket because you will be using it for later.

Wearing the same clothes, right before your performance review, find a quiet spot to sit down and look at that paper. Close your eyes and visualize yourself, getting the raise or the promotion you want. You need to feel the positive energy of those accomplishments and the things you've done wash over you and flow into your body. You can then call out to your guides and ask them to guide you during your review to get the things you have wanted and worked so hard for. This will give you the guidance and positive energy you need to go into that performance review and do great things.

Money and career spells are only as good as your belief and confidence that they will work. You need to invest in your faith in the deities and the guides and trust they would guide you in finding the money and abundance you're looking for, and career advancement and prosperity. Visualization is essential for these spells to work. You have to see yourself getting those things and believe that you can achieve them. Money and career spells are not just about believing in the magic, but it is also about believing in your worth and that you deserve to have those good things happening to you.

Chapter 7: Manifestation Spells

The moon can be so powerful that it can help you get the things you want most in life. If you learn how to harness the moon's energy and power, there is much you can do. The moon can help you improve your health, find love, and find a better, more fulfilling career. The lunar phases can be utilized to such a powerful effect if you understand what you are doing. This is why you need to teach yourself how to align with the different phases and manifestations so you can get everything your heart desires. It takes time and practice, but when you master it, you will have much greater control over your life and the things that manifest within it.

To commit to manifesting with the moon, in this chapter, we will explore manifestation spells that can help you work with the natural forces of the moon and live in sync with all the moon's phases. Be very patient with manifestation because this is a process, and it takes time. Being one with the moon's energy and manifesting the things you want in life isn't something that will happen overnight, and you need to understand that. The best time to perform manifestation spells is when the moon is full.

Full Moon Ritual

The full moon is a time for manifestation and seeing your plans coming to fruition. It is the most powerful time of the lunar cycle and represents completeness and being fulfilled. To manifest with the full moon, we will look at the powerful Full Moon Ritual.

Mindset: The first step of this full moon ritual is to get into the right mindset. This is a part of the lunar cycle when you need to be quiet and reflective, waiting for the actions and intentions you've set earlier to come to a realization. Start by calming your mind and find serenity in your magical space so you can harness the immense power present during this lunar phase. Light a few candles, smudge your magical space with incense, and relax and clear your mind. You cannot manifest with the full moon unless you are in the right mindset.

Reflect: Reflect on the past during this ritual. What has happened over the past few weeks? Are your goals and desires manifesting and coming to fruition? Should you do something different? Look for opportunities for self-improvement and success so you can change the upcoming days. Think about the roadblocks you've faced and the challenges that have slowed you down. This is how you can work on a plan to overcome these challenges and turn things around over the next lunar cycle.

Declaring Intent: By this point of the ritual, know what has worked for you and what has not. So, write down the things slowing you down and the things you want to happen. Take the paper on which you have written down the obstacles blocking your path and burn it or flush it down the toilet. This will help you overcome these obstacles and reach your goals in the future.

Go Outside: Some people call it a moon bath, and it is a peaceful time basking in the full glow of the moon. Either way, go outside and sit under the moonlight. Let it wash over you with its energy and power. It will help you spiritually and physically since the moonlight provides several benefits to our bodies, just like the sunlight. It will also help you relax and focus on your intentions for the next lunar phase.

Dance: There is nothing like dancing to help you manifest and align your powers and energies to those of the moon. Dancing is therapeutic and can help you release any negative energy you still have, so it is a cleanse of sorts. So, dance! It will make you feel better and more relaxed. Dancing under the moon will help you find your spiritual base.

Water Ritual

The second full moon ritual we will discuss is a moon water ritual that can help you manifest, clear your mind, and open your heart. This ritual starts with a mason jar you fill with tap water and then screw on the lid. The tools for this ceremony are simple, as you can see, and it can be done easily, though you need to believe it will work to get the best results.

Take the water jar and put it outside under direct moonlight, and let it stay there overnight--make sure that the lid is on so the water does not become contaminated. Then, after putting it outside, take time to think about and focus on your intents for the next lunar cycle. Think about the things you want to accomplish and how you will do that. In the morning, you can reclaim the jar to do one or more things with it. You can drink a little of the water every day, and every time you take a sip from the moon-blessed water, remind yourself of your intents and goals. This water has the power of the full moon in it and can be very potent.

You can also use this enchanted water to bless your magical tools, especially your crystals. The crystals can absorb magical energies if bathed in moon water, and this will help amplify their powers, making them more potent in your upcoming rituals and spells. Some people use this blessed moon water on their skin as a beauty element. They add it to an oil or cream and then place the beauty product on their faces every day.

This ritual can help you align your energy with that of the moon because the moon's power will accompany you constantly with that blessed water, so use it wisely and keep reminding yourself of your intentions and goals. Manifesting with moon water can bring you closer to your goals and dreams.

Wishes Manifestation Ritual

This ritual is all about harnessing the power of the full moon to manifest your wishes and bring them to life. You will need paper, a pencil, candles, and a box of any shape or material. Start this ritual by listing your manifestations. Let the Goddess guide you, and her power and energy usher you into writing down your manifestations, so you can see them coming to fruition.

Light a candle to start this ritual and focus your thoughts. Let go of negative thoughts in your head and forget about past pains and troubles. Focus on the now and the present moment, releasing other thoughts lingering in your head. Take a moment to think about the things you want to release or get rid of and what you want to attract and invite into your mind and soul. Then, write down on the paper the things you want to invite into your life over the next lunar cycle. List everything and focus on making your intentions pure and realistic. These full moon wishes could be fulfilled by the next lunar cycle, so channel your energy and focus on your intents while writing those wishes down.

Then, place the piece of paper with your wishes in a box or a jar--any container will work here. Take the box or jar and place it outside in the moonlights so it can absorb its energy and bask in the immense power coming from the moon. Like with the previous ritual, in the morning, reclaim the box or the jar and take it into your house. Put it somewhere where you can see it every day. Ideally, it could be your altar, which is already a magic space regularly cleansed and charged. But you could also place the jar on a counter or your nightstand if you wish. Every night, before you go to bed, consider your wishes you want to manifest and think about why you want those things. This will help you realize and manifest those things in the upcoming lunar cycles.

Cleansing Ritual

You can't manifest with the different lunar cycles unless you cleanse yourself and your space. The key to manifestation and realizing your goals is ridding yourself of negative energies and frequencies, which is the purpose of this ritual. You will need a few simple ingredients for this one: incense or herbs like rosemary and juniper. The purpose of this ritual is to use the smoke coming from the burned incense or herbs to purify your home from dark energies, and the full moon is the perfect time to do that. Performing a cleansing ritual like this one during this part of the lunar cycle can purify your home from bad frequencies and lingering negativity.

Light the herbs or incense and then move around the different rooms in your house with the smoke to purify each area as you go. Take advantage of this cleansing ritual to release anything you don't want in your life, too, and get rid of darker thoughts that are no longer serving you and are just slowing you down. Let the moon Goddess guide you in this cleansing ritual as you waft the smoke around the house. Go where you feel the energies are darker or negative and declare out loud that you cleanse this space of any negative influences. Once you're done wafting the smoke, open the windows and let the moonlight wash over your rooms, recharging energy and driving any negative influences out. This helps regenerate your home's energy and leaves you with a cleansed living space free of old energies and filled with new ones.

New Moon Ritual

The new moon is a time for new beginnings, the start of a fresh lunar cycle. You can move away from the past and think about the future, looking forward with positivity instead of focusing on your shortcomings and errors. In this phase of the lunar cycle, you need to consider what you want to come into your life and what you want to let go of. It is the perfect time for reflection and rests and planning for the future. A new moon is not the time for action like other lunar phases, so make no rash decisions. Here's how you can perform a new moon ritual.

Prepare a Space: The first thing you need to do in a new moon ritual is to prepare a sacred space in which you can reflect and rest. So, declutter and get rid of anything that you don't need in your magical space. Next, cleanse your space using incense or oils.

Cleanse Yourself: When it's a new moon before you can start the ritual, you need to cleanse yourself. So, after cleansing your space, take a ritual bath with natural salts and essential oils. Let the water wash away your negative energy and cleanse your body of any impurities. Dim the lights and relax in your ritual bath, meditating and relaxing. You've earned your rest, and this is the time where you can relax in preparation for what is to come.

Ground Yourself: An integral part of this new moon ritual is grounding yourself, and the best way to do that is to have all four natural elements present. They will help ground your magical space and keep you too grounded. The candle represents fire, a water bowl with salt represents the ocean, incense depicts the wind, and natural herbs represent the earth. These elements have a calming effect and can keep you focused and relaxed.

Turn a New Page: Once you're grounded, focus on the connection to the greater energies at work. Tap into the moon's energy and try to harness it. When you feel grounded and connected to the moon and its power, you can then turn a new page, both literally and metaphorically. Take paper (or journal) and start writing. Don't force anything; just let the writing flow out of you and clear your mind as you do so. Write everything you're feeling and thinking at that moment. Declare your intentions and the things you'd like to experience in the weeks to come. When it comes to writing your intentions, be specific because this is how you manifest them. The clearer your intentions are written, the easier it would be for you to manifest them.

Ask for Guidance: After reflecting on your goals and dreams and declaring your intentions, it is time for the final phase of this ritual, which is receiving spiritual guidance. Turn to your deities and guides and ask for help. You can use oracle cards or other magical tools, but it's important to form this connection with your guides so you can trust you are on the right path. Whatever deities or guides you believe in, pray to them and invoke them for guidance and help.

The last step of this ritual is to close your eyes and visualize. Meditate and concentrate on the things you want, and focus on turning a new leaf and starting over. See your intentions manifested and see the things you want in your head. Whatever you want in your life during this lunar cycle, the new moon is the time to think about it and visualize it manifesting. Trust the process, have faith, and it will manifest for you.

Chapter 8: Protection Spells

Whether you want to protect yourself against harm or your loved ones against any evil they might meet in life, protection spells are what you need. This spell is very important when we live where people's intentions and energies are not always pure. This is why you need to have charms and spells in place to keep you and everyone you care about from being harmed.

Energy Cleanse Ritual

The first ritual we will discuss for protecting your home is energy cleanse. It will combine most techniques we have mentioned and help to rid your magical space and the rest of your home. of negative energies and frequencies. You will need several magical tools here, starting with a besom or a broom.

First, you will take the besom or broom and sweep the negative energy out of your house. You must focus on intent, which is clearing the house of any negative energies. Go to every room in the house, moving in a counterclockwise direction, and sweep all the negative energy toward the front door. Start with the ceiling and then move to the corners but don't let the broom touch the walls or floor; you are sweeping energies out of the rooms, not actually sweeping dust. Declare your intent as you move from one room to another, sweeping away all negative energies and declaring that they are not welcome in your space.

After you're done sweeping all negative energies from your space, you will perform a smoke cleanse. You need to burn sage and then move around your house with it to bless the rooms and cleanse any residual negative energies. Like with the sweeping, move in a counterclockwise direction and focus on every room's four corners because this is where negative energy often dwells. The smoke of the sage will help you get rid of any lingering energies, and more important, bless your house with love, wealth, and abundance. Visualize these more positive energies covering your home as you perform this part of the ritual and imagine the negative energy being replaced with the positive one.

After this, you will use a bell to renew the energy of your house. We mentioned earlier how bells could help ward off dark energies; they can also bring peace and harmony to your home, which is always required with such a ritual. While moving with a bell around your home, circle in a clockwise direction to bring in energy. You can chime the bell three times in each room because three is a sacred number. As you ring the bell, declare your intent, and say what energy you want to attract, always repeating positive phrases and chants.

We're toward the end of the ritual now, and this next part is about anchoring and preserving the positive energy you have invited. You will do this by using crystals, which contain immense energy and can stabilize your house's energy levels, keeping them at the level you need and wish to be surrounded by. To anchor the energy in your home, place a crystal in every room; the type of crystal will depend on the energy and vibrations you wish to keep-- crystals have different powers, and you need to put ones that will serve the purpose of the room. You could put a black crystal next to your home's entrance to cleanse any negative energies and offer protection. In your bedroom, you could add rose quartz to promote love and intimacy with your partner. As you move to each room, placing the crystals, move in a clockwise direction, and visualize the energy you wish to infuse with the crystals. Focus on your intent and visualize the crystals carrying this positive energy and anchoring it in each room.

The last step of this ritual, which is to infuse your house with positive energy further, is to go around every room again and draw a pentacle. The pentacle is a symbol of all major elementals, and it can add lots of positive energies to your house. Using a wand or a crystal, move around the rooms in a clockwise direction one last time and draw the pentacle on the doorway ceiling of each room, invoking the deities and the elementals in the process and asking them to offer protection to your home and to bless it.

Doing this ritual, you will have managed to cleanse all dark and negative energies from your home. You will have replaced those with positive energies that will last and offer protection for you and your loved ones.

Protection from Enemies

We always fear pain and torment, whether it is physical or emotional, but unfortunately, it sometimes follows us around no matter what we do, which is usually because of the evil in people and places. With a little help, you can protect yourself and your loved ones from such torment using this Dark or Waning Moon spell--toward the end of the lunar cycle, right before the new moon. This spell is to protect you and the people you care about from an enemy or someone who may wish to do you harm.

To start this spell, make sure you are using a dark altar. Place two candles, one on each side of the altar--one of them needs to be black. After casting your circle, you need to write on the black candle the name of your enemy or the person bringing negative energy. Then, invoke your deities and ask them to help you and protect you and your loved ones. Dip the black candle in the juice of the dieffenbachia plant, which you should prepare beforehand. This juice has the power to numb the tongue, which is to stop your enemy from speaking bad things about you and your loved ones. While dipping the candle in the plant juice, ask the Goddess to stop your enemies from speaking evil about you and request that their tongues be numbed.

You also need spider webs for this spell because you will next roll the candle in the webs and ask the Goddess this person be caught in a web of their deceit rather than harm you or your loved ones. Light the candle after writing the person's name on a piece of paper, and keep praying to the deities to protect your family from all evil and cause this person to face the consequences of their actions. Then, burn the paper with the name, placing it in the black candle's flame, collecting the ashes as they appear. The ashes need to be sprinkled at night in a location where you are certain your enemy will walk, perhaps by their home or place of work. Finally, light the second candle, blue or white, and meditate. This candle signifies the peace and harmony bestowed upon you and your loved ones now that you are safe from your enemy's evil.

Dark Moon Protection Spell

This is another Dark Moon protection spell, which means it needs to be done on the lunar cycle's last day. This spell utilizes a charm bag to protect whomever you want. You can use the spell to protect your children as they grow, your lover at work, or even yourself from evil forces. In simple terms, a charm bag is a pouch that encloses enchanted items that manifest a certain intention, in this case, protection. A charm bag has to be kept on you or worn for some time to see results. While charm bags have often been depicted negatively in movies and TV shows, often claimed to be used by witches to harm others, they are used positively in real life and can help you keep your loved ones safe.

This spell is ideal for the Dark Moon because this time of the month is associated with the Dark Goddess, the Crone. She is known by many names such as Persephone, Lilith, or Hecate. She is the protector and the wise woman, which is why this is the perfect time for banishment and protection spells. In short, this spell can provide you with protection against the darkness out there because it is associated directly with the Dark Goddess.

The best time to perform the spell is during the moon's waning phase or on the Dark Moon itself, right before the New Moon. Try to perform this ritual on a Saturday. You will need a few things for the charm bag, but most of these are easy to find. You should have a maple leaf, a charm bead, black ribbon, lock of hair, Himalayan salt, dragon's blood oil, lavender, nettle, sage, black tourmaline, and a black pouch or piece of cloth in which you will add the ingredients. This spell is performed over two steps, and the second one is a consecration ritual, for which you will need a black candle and incense.

Prepare everything as you sit by your altar, meditating, and getting into the right mindset. Focus on your intent and prepare to cast the protection spell. Cast a magical circle and fill the pouch with the ingredients we've listed (except for the bead and ribbon). Conjure and focus on your intention to be protected or to protect someone you care about from harm. With the pouch filled, thread the protection bead around the black ribbon and seal the pouch with it.

For the second part of this ritual, light the black candle, and invoke the Goddess. Pray to her and ask her to offer you protection and consecrate the charm bag so you can use it to protect yourself or your loved ones against all evil in the world. You can create a chant or use a standard one, but make sure it delivers the true meaning and implores the Goddess for her help in consecrating the charm bag so you can use it for protection. Visualize the protective energy emanating from the pouch and imagine that energy is shielding you or whoever you're making the spell for from any dark energies and all evil. When you're done, praise the Goddess, and snuff the candle, concluding your ritual.

This charm bag should be carried with you or the person you've made it for. It can be worn, put in a bag, or even tucked into your pocket. Just don't move without it, or at the very least, never keep it out of your sight. Remember: nobody else should touch the bag! If that happens, you must perform another ritual to consecrate it. At the end of every lunar cycle, recharge your protection charm by either dosing it with moon water or leaving it under the moon overnight.

Black Salt for Spiritual Protection

Black salt is one of the most common magical ingredients used to offer spiritual protection for your soul and home. It is incredibly useful and efficient in countering the effects of the negativity we encounter in our daily lives. From toxic relationships and exhausting working conditions to your demons and overthinking, negative frequencies are more common in our lives than we would like to admit. This is where black salt comes in. It can absorb the negative energy coming in from all around you and pluck away the dark vibrations troubling you.

So, how do you make it? You need one thing: black pepper, activated charcoal powder, fire pit ashes, or black food coloring. You use one of those with coarse sea salt to make your black salt. To make a more potent black salt, you can also add ingredients like rosemary, cinnamon, lavender essential oil, or cayenne powder. Combine the salt with those and then use the moon's power to charge this combination. You can leave the mix under the light of a dark or a full moon to increase its efficiency and heighten its powers.

Now that you have your black salt, it is time to use it! There is no specific rule on how you should use it, so you can do so however you please. You can sprinkle black pepper around your home to protect you and your loved ones from any darkness or evil. You could also put some in your car to protect you from road trouble or in a small jar at your office to keep away toxic coworkers and the trouble that comes with them.

Chapter 9: Banishing Spells

The last spells we will be discussing in this part is banishing spells, which can be used for a variety of essential purposes. A banishing spell is simply used to get rid of any negative influences in your life, whether those are people or thoughts and feelings you have been struggling with. A banishing spell could relieve you of the pain of a traumatic experience that has long haunted you. You also cast a banishing spell when you want to end a toxic relationship or friendship doing you more harm than good or want a fresh start and let go of the past with all its pain.

Full Moon Release Ritual

While banishing spells are customarily cast during the moon's waning phases, some can be cast during a full moon, as this release ritual. This ritual focuses on tapping into the moon's energy and its natural alignment with our moods and cycles. Our moods change with the change of lunar phases, and your energy levels do, too. This release ritual will help you tap into the full moon's power so you can get rid of anything slowing you down or causing you pain in life. You will need a pen and paper, sage or oils, and candles.

To start this ritual off, you need to cast your magical circle, but first, cleanse your magical circle of any lingering negative energies that might be impeding the ritual. You can put on soothing music to get into the mood and prepare yourself mentally to go through this ceremony. Clear your mind of all thoughts and focus your energies. You can also burn candles and incense to help you focus and channel your energy. The candles will also cleanse the space of dark vibrations and negative energy. Visualize all bad energies seeping away from your body and leaving you to meditate calmly under the moonlight.

Then, ground yourself and take control of your body and breathing. After meditating, you must learn of the moment and of how you are feeling. Think about the things you would like to release from your life and why you wish to do so. It could be a job causing you pain and exhaustion or a relationship weighing you down and affecting your life negatively. Whatever it is, write it down on a piece of paper and declare your intent to get rid of this negative effect on your life. Then, sign your name on the paper and date it. Finally, close your eyes, and declare to the universe you are releasing whatever it is that is troubling you from your life. Visualize this happening and have faith that the universe will handle everything.

After that, hold the paper with your hand over the lit candle and let the flame burn away your troubles and release the negativity. Visualize the smoke of the burning paper declaring your intentions to the universe and helping you find peace and harmony. You must end this ritual on a positive note. Meditate and clear your mind of thoughts about the negative thing you have released, and be grateful. Sit in peace and silence for a while, and be grateful for the things you have learned from those tough situations or toxic people. Forgive those that have wronged you and let go of any hatred or negativity you have toward them--this could also mean forgiving yourself for any pain you might have caused. You've released whatever it is that was troubling you, so there's no point in dwelling on the loss and pain.

Express your gratitude toward the universe for helping you release those troubles and thank the deities for helping you wash those troubles away. Finally, take a ritual cleansing bath to calm yourself and wash away any remaining negativity.

Spell to Banish Negativity

No matter how hard we try, the mind has its way of dwelling on the negative things affecting you. You can try hard to have positive thoughts and not dwell on what's hurting you, but sometimes, the negative thoughts are just too powerful. This spell will help you deal with such problems, and you can banish ideas from your mind.

You need a cauldron, pen, red candle, and two pieces of paper for this banishing spell. You can perform this spell during the waning or new moon phases, but never during the waxing moon. Start by drawing a picture of yourself with the dark thoughts weighing you down. There is no right way to do this because it is up to your interpretations and feelings. Maybe you want to draw a picture of yourself with a black cloud hanging over your head or a picture of someone sobbing. Whatever you are feeling, draw it. Then, take the red candle and charge it with the moon's energy because it will have a healing effect for this spell. After that, light the candle and hold the tip of the picture you have drawn in the flame.

When the picture catches fire, place it in the cauldron. Then, draw another picture of yourself, this time happy and without the negativity weighing you down. Take this second picture and place it under the red candle. Then, let the candle burn out as you visualize yourself releasing whatever is bothering you and enjoying a happier life, all with the moon's light washing over you and recharging your energy.

Four Thieves Vinegar to Banish Evil

This is one of the most popular potions to banish evil and negativity, and its origin dates back hundreds of years. You will need lavender, rosemary, sage, thyme, mint, apple cider vinegar, garlic, and a jar or airtight container for this spell. You should also choose fresh herbs for this spell.

Start by putting the herbs inside the jar and then cover the herbs with apple cider vinegar and close the lid tightly. Store it in a cool and dry place, and give the jar a gentle shake every day for 1 to 1.5 months. Then, take the herbs out of the vinegar, and your potion is ready to use. There are several ways to use the four thieves vinegar, and it will help you banish all evil and ward yourself or your loved ones against the dark forces at work in the world.

You can sprinkle this vinegar around your doorstep to keep dark energies and evil out and to protect your home from enemies. If you don't mind the taste, it can also be used as an ingredient in cooking to provide you with protection and banish all evil around you as you move, plus break spells that might be cast upon you.

Spell to Banish Depression

Stress and depression are the plagues of modern humans. Whether it is the stresses of your daily job or depression from existential crises and not knowing your purpose in life, this spell might just help. You've already probably tried every other approach to making yourself feel better and getting rid of your stress and sadness, and it might just be time to try something different.

For this spell, you will need a black stone and a candle. This spell requires going to a body of running water, preferably during the new or waning moon, so find the nearest stream, brook, or even ocean. Sit down, light the candles, and hold the stone in your right hand. Calm yourself and meditate. Think about all the things weighing you down and causing depression and stress. Channel those thoughts and negative energies into the stone you are holding. When you feel those troubles and pains have left your body and settled into the stone, toss it into the water and chant. Declare to the Goddess and the universe you wish for those feelings and thoughts to have left your body, and you wish them to be replaced with peace, serenity, and happiness.

After doing so, ground and calm yourself, sit and dwell on the feelings you are experiencing, and how good it feels to be rid of those dark thoughts and the depression. Thank the Goddess for her help in relieving your pain. Stay for a while at the body of running water and let the moon's energy wash over you and rid you of any remnants of negativity and depression. Then, blow out the candles, pack up, and go home, believing that your depression is a thing of the past.

Reflective Banishing

We all have people and things in our lives that are a source of constant stress and pain, and they can channel their negative energy towards you so you often find yourself unable to resist being affected by the negativity. This spell is for this situation; it's designed to reflect this negativity at the target, whether it is a toxic person in your life or unwanted spirits causing you a lot of pain. You need a small mirror and something to write with (an oil pencil works perfectly here).

Write down the name of the person or spirit causing you pain and declare underneath the name you henceforth send back and reflect this dark energy. Add a banishing symbol too. Then, carry the mirror around with you until this person or spirit has ceased channeling their negativity your way.

Spell to Remove Curses

This next spell is all about removing curses from an object. If you have an object you believe is cursed, this spell could help. Removing curses often depends on the curse's strength, but you need to try several approaches until it is lifted. Try a purification ritual to remove a curse from an object; you can do that by dipping the object in saltwater and then lighting incense and letting its smoke cover the item -- you can also use holy water instead of incense. If the curse is weak, it will be removed by this simple purification ritual. If it is strong, you might need to do something else.

Until you know exactly the curse on the item, you need to at least limit its harms so you could do a counter-spell. You can do so by putting a copper item on the object since copper is capable of drawing negative energies and maintaining a certain balance of the object's energy. This is a temporary solution, though. Your best chance knows what curse has been placed on this item so you could perform a particular ritual or cast a certain spell that works with this specific curse. Copper can only draw negative energies for so long, and it might fail so this is not a long-term solution to this problem. If you do encounter a cursed object, follow a certain order. Start with the cleansing ritual and pray it works and removes the curse. If it doesn't, try to learn as much as you can about the curse and understand what exactly it can do. Until you do so, use a coin or any other copper object to dampen the effects of the curse and reduce its harm.

Spell to Banish Danger

This is a very important spell for banishing dangerous people you might have crossed paths with and feared for your life or that of your loved ones. It will help you banish the danger and protect everyone and everything you care about. You will need a red ribbon, poppet (doll) to represent the person (or persons) that are dangerous, a black candle, and myrrh incense.

Cast your magical circle and light the incense and the black candle. Put salt water on the poppet and declare your intentions towards this person. You want them to stay away from you and your loved ones, so declare it and bless the poppet for this chant to work. Then, hold the doll in your hand and visualize it bound by a silver net, representing the dangerous person being bound from ever hurting you. After that, use the red ribbon to tie the poppet up tightly, making sure you bind it so it cannot do you any harm.

After binding the poppet, charge it by chanting to the Gods and Goddesses and honoring the elements. Declare that you wish this poppet and who it represents to be bound and their harm banished from you and everyone you care about. This marks the conclusion of the spell. Open your circle and take the poppet and bury it. Bury it under a waning moon, bury it far from your home, and put a heavy rock over its burial place. This will help banish the danger this person brings and will protect you and your family from their evil.

Spell to Remove People from Your Life

The next spell we will discuss is to banish unwanted people from your life. You will need sea salt, black and white candles, a picture of yourself, and a quartz stone to perform this spell.

Cast a circle of the sea salt and put the quartz stone, the white candle, and your picture inside it. Bless the white candle and demand it protects only you from any possible harm. Then, light it. After that, take the black candle and bless it to absorb all negative energies that might affect you. Light this black candle and place it outside the salt circle and let it burn out. This will help protect you from any negative energies and keep that person away from you until they are removed from your life.

Spell to Banish Alcohol Addiction

Struggling with alcohol addiction is one of the worst challenges a person can find themselves in. Unfortunately, it happens often without you even noticing. You tell yourself it will be just a glass or two to take the edge off or relax after a long and stressful day, and you could soon find yourself addicted to that numbing sensation that alcohol gives you. In these tough times, you could do a spell to banish this addiction and help you stop drinking alcohol.

For this spell, get around a dozen pieces of small paper, a pen or pencil, black string or cord, a glass of water, amethyst crystal, and an empty bottle of your favorite alcohol, but it needs to have a lid, and wash it before this spell. Before you begin the ritual, think about why you want to stop drinking alcohol. Whatever those reasons were, write them down on a piece of paper, separately. You need to be honest with yourself here, so write down the reasons as they are, whether you're hurting the people you love, affecting your job, or anything.

Next, cast your magic circle as you usually do and meditate for a while. Calm yourself and clear your mind; you must have untroubled thoughts for this ritual to work. Then, pick up a piece of paper and read what is on it out loud and then declare its opposite also aloud. For instance, if the paper said, "I argue with my wife a lot because I drink alcohol," then you need to affirm its opposite and say, "I don't fight with my wife as much now because I stopped drinking alcohol." Visualization is key for this ritual to work. You need to imagine yourself freed from the burden of alcohol abuse and without a care on your mind now that you are sober. Believe that the things you are reading out loud are true, and they will come to be.

Think about how it would feel if it were true, and you were free from this addiction and healthy, leading a better life. Take the piece of paper you've read and put it in the empty bottle. Then, pick up another piece of paper and repeat the process. Once you have finished them all, put the lid on and close the bottle with the papers inside. Take the black string or cord, tie it around the bottle's neck, and do three knots (remember the importance of the number 3). Next, take the glass of water, let the moonlight shine on it, washing it over with its energy. And drink water. Visualize this water cleansing you and purifying you of the need for alcohol.

Finally, take the crystal and put it in your hands, and sit in the moonlight. Feel the light covering you with its power and let it flow from you to the crystal. Meditate on getting rid of your alcohol addiction and becoming sober, all while holding the crystal. Then, declare it to the universe; say you are not a drinker anymore, and it shall be true. Close the circle and meditate for a while. Then, take the bottle and get rid of it; you can bury it in the ground or just throw it away. After the ritual, remember to carry the crystal with you. If you ever feel the urge to drink alcohol, drink water, and visualize as you did before, just believe it will work.

Spell to Banish Negative Influences

Finally, we will discuss a candle banishing ritual to help you get rid of negative influences in your life. For this, you need a black candle and a candle holder, salt, a carving tool, like a pin or sharp knife, black or white pepper, and an anointing oil of any kind.

Start by sprinkling the salt in a counterclockwise direction to form a circle around yourself. As you sprinkle it, visualize the salt-forming a protective shield around you and your magical space to protect you from any dark forces. Think about your banishing spell's goal and what you wish to get rid of, be it is a person or a feeling. Then, declare your intent by carving this desire into the candle, like wishing to lose your anxiety or exhaustion or wanting someone never to cross your path ever again. It is also a good idea to carve a banishing sigil or symbol into the candle.

When you're done, use the oil to anoint the candle and also sprinkle it with salt. Then, place the candle in the holder and light it while declaring your intentions out loud. Let the candle burn out as you sit down next to it and meditate, visualizing your desires coming to fruition and whatever you want out of your life being banished. After you are done, break the circle and forget about the spell.

Section 3: Other Ways to Work with the Moon

Chapter 10: Moon Water, Crystals, and Oils

By now, you understand many spells that you can cast with the moon's power, but there are still many ways through which you can harness that power and use it to your advantage. The energy that comes from the moon over the lunar cycle can bless many items and charge your magical items with energy. In this chapter, we will explore other ways to use the power coming from the moon, whether it is to create moon water or to consecrate your crystals and work with oils. These techniques can be done separately, or they can be done together to maximize your harvesting of the moon's energy.

Moon Water

We gave detailed instructions in a previous chapter about how to create moon water, but that is not the only way it can be crafted. Some prefer to make moon water during the new and full moon phases, only to be used in special magical rituals and at specific times throughout the lunar cycles. Others make moon water during the waxing or the waning lunar phases. It all depends on your preferences, connection to the moon, and the time you think is ideal for working on this ritual. Here is a simple guide on how you can make moon water, but you can follow a different approach if you please.

1. Preparing the Container

The first step to making moon water is preparing a container reflective of not just who you are as a person but also what you are trying to attract. If you are trying to attract wealth, you can use a more expensive vessel. You could also use a mason jar of any kind, but it needs to be charged with your intent and your goals for the next lunar cycle so you can use it to the maximum efficiency.

2. Charge the Container

While don't do this step, it is beneficial if you do. Charging the container before you perform the moon ritual can help ward off any negative energies that might be lingering around and draining your energy or infusing you with negative vibrations. You can use crystals for this purpose because they have healing effects and can help protect you from negative energies and unwelcome influences.

3. Put the Container Under the Moonlight

With the container ready, fill it with water. You should use a jar or container with a lid to avoid having anything contaminating your moon water. Then, take the jar and put it under the moonlight during the phase you feel will be best to charge your water--ideally, it should be a full or a new moon. While you should put the jar under direct moonlight outside, if you live in an apartment and this will be complicated, you can put the container by a window.

4. Retrieve the Container

After leaving the jar overnight, retrieve it in the morning with your newly-charged moon water. Keep your moon water with you because there are many ways you can use it.

Water Elemental in Rituals: The first way you can use the moon water is in your magical rituals. Put moon water in a chalice, place it on the altar, and it can be a representation of the water element during your rituals. You can use this chalice of moon water to call the quarters, too.

Offerings: Moon water can be an offering to the deities. It is the perfect offering to the deities you invoke, and it can help you summon their guidance and blessing. Put some of it in a bowl along with flowers or petals, or whatever offer you think your deities would appreciate. After that, present the offering to your deity with a chant or a prayer of your making.

Blessing and Charging: You can use the moon water to bless any magical items you use during your rituals and spells. You can use it, for instance, to bless the pen with which you will write in your book of shadows or bless your wand or any other magical items you will use during rituals. Moon water can charge and cleanse your altar and all your magical tools. To consecrate a magical item with moon water, dip a finger in the moon charged water and then draw a pentacle or other magical symbols on the items you want to bless.

Charging crystals in moon water is one of the most common practices for witches as it regenerates and charges the crystals' powers, and you can then use them for cleansing rituals and other magical spells and ceremonies. The combination of crystals and moon water can be powerful if used correctly.

Anointing: Moon water is often used to anoint objects and not just magical ones. For example, you can anoint your money with moon water to promote wealth and attract good fortune. This is because water as an element is often associated with money, as both flows. For such a ritual, focus on your intents and be specific to the wealth you'd like to attract. Imagine the wealth and abundance flowing in your direction, much as water would.

Cleansing: Always remember that moon water can cleanse your home of any negative energies and dark vibrations.

Beauty and Self-Care: A lot of witches use moon water for beauty purposes. You can wash your face with it or add it to beauty products. You can add moon water to your bath to recharge your body and cleanse it while you're bathing. You can also use it in vases with flowers to give your flowers a blessed life.

Promoting Creativity: Moon water is believed to boost and promote creativity. You can clean your workspace with moon water and even wipe your vision board with it. You can use moon water with your chakras to promote psychic abilities and creativity.

These are just ways to use moon water; essentially, you can use it in whatever way you want. From cooking to cleaning, this charged water can give you positive energy and cleanse you of bad vibrations, plus bless your home.

Crystals

Crystals can be used with moon energy to a great effect, but you need to know what crystals to work with and how. The challenge with crystals is that there are many types out there, and you need to select the right kind to work with and in the proper moon phase, or else your intention won't come to manifest. Here are crystals you can use to harvest and channel the moon's energy.

Moonstone

While it may sound a little obvious, the moonstone is one of the best crystals to work with the moon's energy. You don't need a particular color of moonstone; it could be white or even black. The best thing about this crystal is that you can use it to work with lunar energy during all moon phases, so you're not bound to the new or full moons, though its power on the full moon is extremely potent. If you feel that power while wearing it on a full moon and do not like the amount of power you feel, you can put it aside until the moon's next phase with no adverse effects.

The moonstone resembles the Goddess and the feminine energy that comes with her, which is not surprising considering the moon itself manifests the Goddess and divine feminine energy. Use the moonstone to tap into your intuition and channel your gut feelings to help manifest your desires. Whenever you want to align with your goals, and tap into your power, use the moonstone during any moon phase.

Selenite

Selenite is one of the most popular crystals for many witches, and for a good reason. Its power is great, and it's used to do many great things. The name of the crystal is derived from the Moon Goddess Selene, and it is a full moon crystal, so it is best utilized during this lunar phase to make the most out of the lunar energy. There is a certain iridescence to selenite that is like the moon's shine, and it is believed this crystal emanates peace and joy to those who use it.

Selenite can help you process the range of emotions and fears that often manifest with the full moon, which is why it is best used during this part of the lunar cycle. It can neutralize and repel the negative energies that often surround us and bring us down. While this crystal is used to repel dark energies and emit positive vibrations, it could still need cleaning occasionally so you can get the best outcome while using it. You need to charge your selenite under the full moon by leaving it at night to bask in the energy of the moon.

When you use selenite, focus on your intentions and on repelling negative energies. Also visualize this crystal, bringing you joy and happiness and manifesting good things in your life.

Labradorite

There is a certain shimmer of changing color to Labradorite under certain light, which makes it look beautiful and captivating. This crystal has protective qualities and can offer you protection against negative energy and dark vibrations. This crystal is best used during the full moon and is great for manifestation rituals. Labradorite is also believed to be linked to the sun's energy, which gives it an even greater power considering it has both sources of energy linked to it.

This particular crystal is used to help you find balance in your life and in figuring out what is slowing you down. What are you not confronting? What is stopping you from moving to a better place and leading a better life? These are all questions that can be answered using Labradorite since it boosts spirituality and intuition and can help connect you with yourself and your innermost feelings. Labradorite is a crystal of spiritual awakening and transformation, and after using it with the full moon, you can transform your life.

Amethyst

Amethyst is not necessarily used with or linked to the full moon, but it can benefit greatly from its energy. This violet stone vibrates at a special frequency that can be amplified by the full moon. Amethyst can help you overcome the heavy feelings that might be weighing you down, and it can help you navigate your inner turmoil to come out feeling better about yourself and your insecurities.

Amethyst can keep you grounded, boosts spirituality, and puts you in direct contact with your intuition so you can figure out what is bothering you and causing you to feel unhappy. Use this crystal during different lunar cycles, but the full moon most of all, to overcome your insecurities and fears and come to terms with your shortcomings.

Opal

Opal is one of the most powerful crystals you can use during the moon phases. Its strength comes from its connection to the water element, which, as we mentioned several times, is closely associated with the moon's energy. Opal represents purification and is a manifestation of the cleansing of dark energies around your home. Use it to bless your magical tools and altar and to cleanse your home before casting your magical circle.

Clear Quartz

It is believed that clear quartz contains power and knowledge that can bless your moon rituals with powerful protection. The great thing about clear quartz is its versatility, and it is considered one of the most commonly used crystals. You can use it for any purpose, depending on your intentions.

It can be used during the full moon phase to channel your intent toward positive energies and attracting better things to your life. Clear quartz can help you align your energy with that of the moon, so you can declare your intentions to the world and see them coming to fruition.

Moon Oil

Moon oil can increase the power of your intentions and channel certain energies. You can carry it around to repel dark energies and cleanse yourself. Moon oil has herbs and oils blessed with the lunar energy and can help you harness that energy.

To make moon oil, you can choose the oil you like best or believe will fit most with what you need the oil for. If you plan on using moon oil on your skin, it might be worth getting skin-friendly oils and won't irritate. If that is not your intent, then you could use any oils you want to work with. For the intents of this part, we will use grapeseed oil and sweet almond or avocado oil. You can add essential oils like rose or jasmine oil. Add herbs to the mixture--

you can choose herbs you think will help you harness the moonlight. Use a small bottle to combine the mixture and use it whenever you need it.

After you put everything in the bottle, add small crystals too to charge the mixture with even more potent energy. Leave the bottle under the moon overnight to charge during any of the moon phases, perhaps the full moon for the greatest power. Collect it in the morning as you would with moon water and use the moon oil however you please.

Chapter 11: Moon Goddess Rituals

In this chapter, we will explore rituals you can perform to honor the Moon Goddess. As you now know, she has been known by many names across various civilizations, all having their ways of honoring her. To this day, several religious traditions still honor the Moon Goddess and conduct rituals in her honor. Some must be done during certain phases of the lunar cycle where her presence is most noted, and others during any part of the cycle.

Drawing Down the Moon Ritual

This is a powerful and beautiful Wiccan ritual to invoke the Moon Goddess. The witch casting this spell invokes the Goddess into herself, drowning into a trance-like state, to speak the words of the Goddess and relay her commands. This ritual is best practiced during the full moon or right before it, and it is best done outdoors so you can be in direct contact with the moon's energy, but if that is impossible, you can do it indoors but make sure you are in a clear view of the moon.

There is not a single right way to do this ritual, and different witch will have varying approaches. It will depend on your personal beliefs and how you generally practice your magic. You will need a cleansed altar for this ritual, so start by clearing the magical space of all negative energies and evil spirits. After cleansing the place with sage or crystals, stand before your altar, facing the full moon, and cross your arms. While in this position, invoke the Moon Goddess. You can use whichever phrasing or chanting you are comfortable with. Just pray to and invoke the Goddess's presence into your sacred magical space.

Raise your arms and move your feet to be shoulder's width apart. By opening your arms like this, you are welcoming the Goddess into your mortal vessel. You will feel your energy fluctuating, and power will surge into your body, which is fine because this is the Moon Goddess entering into you. Speak from your mind on behalf of the Moon Goddess. Declare your presence and your intent and identify yourself as her. There aren't exact words you should chant here; just say what you believe that the Goddess represents and feel her power course through your veins as she takes your body. Honor her and declare your loyalty and undying gratitude to the Goddess, as one should.

To conclude the ceremony, meditate as you feel the power dissipating and the Goddess leaving your body. This is the time to be in a contemplative mood and think about this wonderful thing you have just experienced. Lower your arms to mark the end of the ritual and close the magic circle. You can expect to have heightened powers over the next few days, which is normal; you had a Goddess within you. You might also have sharpened psychic abilities for a few days, so try to look into your future and focus on your intent and the things you would like to invite to your life. The more focused you are, the more you can tap into any residual power that might be in your body and use it to your advantage.

Invoking Artemis (Full Moon Ritual)

This second ritual we will be talking about is invoking the Goddess of Hunt and the Moon Artemis; you will perform this ritual on a full moon. It is similar in objective to the "drawing the moon" ritual because it aims to draw the deity to occupy your body and speak through you, but this one is geared specifically at the Goddess of the hunt. Artemis was believed to be the protector of virgins and all that is chaste, and the forest and wild animals. She was a huntress unlike any other, chaste, beautiful, and pure, also known as the eternal virgin never touched by man or god. This ritual is to honor and pay tribute to her.

For this ritual, you will need a white candle, moonstone crystal, olive oil, mugwort, tarragon, wormwood; you can use only one herb, a combination, or all three. You will also need to prepare shamanic music for the ritual. You need to get into the right mindset before you start this ritual because you are inviting the powerful Goddess Artemis into your body, so you have to be ready. Start by cleansing yourself so you will be receptive to such a powerful deity. Take a ritual cleansing bath to cleanse yourself and become pure to welcome the purest of the Goddesses.

Next, your magical space needs to be cleansed to welcome Artemis. Use smudge or oils to cleanse your magical space, starting at the corners. After cleansing yourself and the location, it is time to start your ritual. Dim the lights, light the incense, and let the candles burn too. Put on shamanic music to prepare your mind and soul and help you dive into a focused meditative state. Cast your magical circle after preparing all the items and ingredients for this ritual.

While listening to the music and enjoying the incense and the setting, allow yourself to dive into a deep meditative state and drift off to a different time and space. Imagine yourself in Artemis's favorite location, a forest in ancient times where trees are everywhere, and wild animals roam freely. Visualizing these scenes is important because it makes for an inviting setting for the Goddess to make her presence known. Then, anoint your white candle with the olive oil and as you do so, honor Artemis and say a prayer for the Goddess. Dedicate this ritual and the burning of the candle to her purity and wild ferocity. After anointing the candle, you need to do the same to yourself with more olive oil, starting from the bottom and moving to the top.

While anointing yourself, it is time to invoke Artemis. You can say words of your choice here, but make sure they are from the heart and carry the honor and veneration that such a Goddess deserves. Invoke the Goddess and ask her to occupy your body and use it as a vessel to bless you with her energy. Call out her name and honor her with the descriptions and titles passed across generations. Then, sprinkle the herbs over yourself and around the candle, honoring the Goddess. Anoint the moonstone, too, and carry it with you. You can wear it as a pendant or put it in your pocket; just make sure it is on you because this crystal represents your connection to the goddess and will ease her passage into your physical form.

Now, it is time to dance! Get up on your feet and dance wildly and freely as the ancient priests did in honor of Artemis. This is the best way to honor the Goddess's pure energy and wild nature, and you need to dance until you can't dance anymore. When your energy has drained, lay back on the floor and let Artemis's energy wash over you and charge you. Slowly sit up once you feel you are blessed with her powers and break the circle. Ground yourself and center. Think about the experience of being one with the Goddess of the hunt and what that means.

You can prepare an altar for Artemis to have her always present with you, blessing you with her ferocity and purity to face whatever you face in life. Set an altar for her with herbs and a white candle, and offer a tribute to Artemis, such as moon water or another magical item.

Full Moon Ritual for Diana

We talked early in the book about the Goddess Diana and how she was considered the triple Goddess and a manifestation of the moon. This ritual is to honor her and to honor the moon's divine feminine power. Diana has often been considered a representation of fertility and feminine power, and she is often invoked in rituals promoting childbirth and relating to women. This ritual is not to invoke Diana to occupy your body but to honor her and form a connection with the Moon Goddess. This is why this is done when the moon is at the peak of its power.

Start by setting up your altar. You don't have to cleanse your altar or space here, but it is often recommended that you do so to connect with Diana clearer and purer. Start with a cleansing ritual, then write down your desires and intents for the future and prayers for the Goddess of the moon on a piece of paper. Take this paper (or cloth) and tie it to a tree. Ask the Goddess to protect you and your loved ones as she protects animals and anyone who worships her and believes in her powers.

Then, back at your altar, continue praying to Diana and ask her to fulfill your wishes and help you find happiness and joy in life. Light a white candle on your altar and offer a bowl of moon water or milk to the Goddess as an offering. Visualize the Goddess helping you get what you want and blessing your life and the life of those you care about. Have faith that Diana can help you get the things you want and meditate on her presence during that full moon. Thank the Goddess for her presence and honor her before you break the magical circle.

Wiccan Esbat

For Wiccans, the Esbat is when they meet on a full moon to celebrate it and honor the Moon Goddess and other deities. They practice magic and express gratitude for the deities that have guided them over the previous lunar cycle. There are approximately 13 Esbats during a year, corresponding to 13 full moons. The Esbat is a time of spirituality and is used to channel the moon's energy to cleanse yourself and achieve your goals. It is also a time for honoring the deities and manifesting their blessing and energies.

While the Wiccan rituals for the sun (Sabbats) have certain meanings, this is not the case with the Esbat. It is about connecting with the moon's energy and using it to change and better your life. This is why there is no right way to practice magic during the Esbats. You just do what your gut feeling tells you and honor the moon and the Goddess; however you want. It can be as simple as going to your backyard during the full moon and meditating under the moonlight and visualizing good things happening.

So, how do you go about a Wiccan Esbat? The most important thing you need to focus on at first is your intention. The Esbat is all about plotting a goal and performing the ritual to promote that goal and honor it. Whether it is to honor the deities, connect with the moon, or to ask the Gods and Goddesses to help you with a personal dream or desire, Esbat is the time to do it. Just be specific about what you want so you can make the most out of Esbat. While Esbats are traditionally performed on a full moon, you could perform the ritual on any part of the lunar cycle if it coincides with your goals--remember we said phases work better for protection spells while others are more suited toward wealth or abundance. So, whatever you want from Esbat, write it down and consider your lunar calendar to find the ideal moment.

Next comes the preparation. You have now defined your goals and what you want to accomplish through the ritual, and you have a time on which you will perform it. After that comes the research. Understand what you need to do for Esbat to work and the ingredients you will need for this spell or ritual. Is it a manifestation spell? Or do you want to attract wealth or love? Perhaps you wish to protect your loved ones against evil and dark energies or promote your fertility so you can conceive. Whatever it is, research the spell and the ritual and prepare the magical tools and ingredients you will need to make it work.

Finally, perform your ritual. As we mentioned, there isn't a specific way to perform the Esbat or a particular objective, so do as your heart tells you. It is not a bad idea; however, to follow practices like cleansing your magical space and yourself so you can correctly honor the deities and perform a proper ritual. Meditate on your intents and visualize them coming to fruition, and you will have made a successful Esbat.

Chapter 12: Creating Your Own Unique Moon Rituals

In this final chapter, we will explore ways through which you can make your unique moon rituals. The beauty of moon spells and rituals is there isn't any handbook on how they must be performed. There are just guidelines and tips to help you on this spiritual and majestic journey, and this leaves a lot of room for improvisation and adding your unique touch to make the rituals and spells more aligned with your beliefs and practices. You don't have to buy the ingredients you use for spells and rituals we've mentioned earlier; you could just make your own!

At the end of the day, moon rituals are about finding your voice and working with something with which you are comfortable. Your energy and beliefs drive these rituals and spells and are the reason they work. So, let's dive into things you could do to make your unique moon rituals.

Unique Full Moon Ritual

Considering how the full moon is the most powerful of the lunar phases where the moon is at the height of its power, it makes sense we start with tips and ideas on how you can create a unique moon ritual personal to you and unlike any other.

Personalize: This is a full moon ritual, and for it to work, you need to keep it simple and personal. The purpose of this ritual is to align your energy with that of the moon, and for that to happen, you need to be authentic. Think about the practices that mean the most to you and try to infuse them within the ritual. Do you like dancing? Then why not include it in your full moon ritual? Maybe meditating is more your thing, so incorporate that. The ritual is an extension of who you are and the things you enjoy, so whatever you like, make sure to make it a part of the ritual.

Prepare the Tools: You need to prepare the tools you will use to complete the spell or perform the ceremony. Again, this will also depend on your preferences. Perhaps there are certain herbs or a sage you prefer to use. Or you might prefer essential oils. Select a crystal or a unique stone of importance to you. Put on the music that works best for you and puts you in a meditative mood; it could be heavy metal or African drums. Experimentation is key here. Keep trying different things. They might work, or they might not. The important thing is they are yours and express who you are as a person.

Sacred Space: After preparing the tools you want to use for this ritual or spell, you need to prepare a sacred space to do your magic. There isn't a rule that says a sacred space should look like this or that, but traditionally it should contain an altar. The altar's importance is that it gives this space sacred importance and lets you know that it is special, different from day-to-day objects, and not an ordinary table.

You can choose whatever location you please in your home to prepare this sacred space, and you can decorate it however you want, too. The most important thing is you being comfortable and feeling like you can freely express yourself in this space. Then. Cleanse this space you have created and remove any dark energies.

Get into the Mindset: What separates a magical ritual from any other thing you do daily is your mindset. With your tools and magical space ready, prepared according to your preferences, you need to next meditate and prepare your mind for a deep spiritual connection to the moon. Think about the things you want to carry out through this ritual and why you are doing this. Then, take time for gratitude and appreciating all the things you have been blessed with. Thank the Moon Goddess for blessing your life and giving you many things to be thankful for. Gratitude is a very important practice that makes it a lot easier for you to establish a genuine connection with the moon's energy.

Toward the end of this ritual, you may do what you feel like doing to conclude the ritual. Some witches like to journal and write down whatever they are feeling, whether it is desires or fears. Or you could affirm your intent and declare how you want the next lunar cycle to be. You could also go outdoors and bathe in the moonlight and let its healing energy wash over you. Close your ritual once you feel like it has served its purpose. You can do so by meditating again, saying a prayer to the Goddess, singing or chanting, dancing, or ringing a bell and saying moon salutations.

New Moon Ritual

The new moon marks new beginnings, and it is a time to set intentions and work on manifesting them. During this very special time of the lunar cycle, you can create a home ritual to celebrate, and it could be a new ritual. You can practice it alone, or you could invite friends or other witches to join in on the new moon ritual to make it more potent.

Before you start this ritual, make sure the magical space you are performing it in is beautiful. Again, this will depend on what you find beautiful, so take liberties in decluttering and adding aesthetic elements that make the sacred space look beautiful to you. Get rid of the things you don't need and set up your altar in a pure and visually pleasing way. You can use objects from around your home to prepare the altar or earth elements from the soil around your home. Anything can work if you believe in it. Put these items on the altar and decorate it however you want.

For this unique ritual, you can ground yourself. Grounding is a healthy practice you can do regardless of any moon rituals. Grounding is best done near a body of water and barefoot so you can feel the energy of the earth and the water. Make your way to the water and let it cover you--you could go all into the water or just dip your feet. Breathe deeply under the moonlight and visualize your intentions manifesting. Let the cold water ground you and anchor your mind and body. Think about your desires and imagine them coming to be.

You could then choose to conclude this unique ritual in many ways. You could write or journal like with the previous ritual. Document your feelings during this new moon and what you want to attract, and what you wish to release from your life. Declare your intentions for this lunar cycle and what you wish to experience. You could then take the piece of paper with your desires and bury it in the garden or set alight to it with a candle, letting your desires become known to the universe and trusting that it will guide your intentions. To wrap things up, burn sage of your choosing or incense to cleanse the space after declaring your intentions.

Tips for Creating Your Rituals

The key to creating a unique ritual is to think about the things that feel magical to you and only you. No rule says you cannot use handmade objects or custom tools to perform magical rituals and invoke deities. Customize the spells and the chants however you please. The Moon Goddess will not care which chant you use to invoke her and ask for her blessing if you honor her and pay her respect. So, try different things in your rituals and see what works best for you. Does yoga relax you and put you in a meditative state of mind? Then, by all means, incorporate yoga into your magical rituals and start or conclude the ceremony by practicing it.

Conclusion

Customize your moon ritual so it makes you feel comfortable and at ease. Your connection with the moon is special and can be felt only by you. Different things might work with other people, so don't worry about copying anyone else, thinking about the elements you find magical, and adding them to your rituals. Harness the moon's energy using tools that others may not find magical; it doesn't matter. Magic is what you decide is magical. Experiment with your rituals and try combining new things on the different lunar phases. You might just find spells and rituals that could change your life for the better. Remember that you should never despair when it comes to creating your unique ritual. Some will work; others will not. You need to stay patient and keep experimenting until you find the right combination of items and rituals. It is much more rewarding because you can perform rituals you have made yourself and are personal to you, which could make the spells much more potent and help you achieve the results you want.

Here's another book by Mari Silva that you might like

Your Free Gift (only available for a limited time)

Thanks for getting this book! If you want to learn more about various spirituality topics, then join Mari Silva's community and get a free guided meditation MP3 for awakening your third eye. This guided meditation mp3 is designed to open and strengthen ones third eye so you can experience a higher state of consciousness. Simply visit the link below the image to get started.

https://spiritualityspot.com/meditation

References

B. A., H., Facebook, F., & Twitter, T. (n.d.). *10 Lunar Gods & Goddesses You Should Know.* Learn Religions. https://www.learnreligions.com/lunar-deities-2562404

Five Spell-Casting Essentials for Beginner Witches. (n.d.). Exemplore. https://exemplore.com/wicca-witchcraft/Witchcraft-For-Beginners-The-Five-Essential-Parts-of-Casting-Spells

Glamour. (n.d.). *Making "moon rituals" can totally enhance your life, here's your ultimate guide.* Glamour UK. Retrieved from https://www.glamourmagazine.co.uk/article/moon-ritual-guide

How to Prepare For a Spell. (2020, March 9). Wishbonix. https://www.wishbonix.com/how-to-prepare-for-a-spell/

M. A., L., & B. A., L. (n.d.). *12 Ancient Lunar Luminaries.* ThoughtCo. https://www.thoughtco.com/moon-gods-and-moon-goddesses-120395

Moon Rituals for Guiding Intentions. (n.d.). Www.Kelleemaize.com. Retrieved from https://www.kelleemaize.com/post/moon-rituals-for-guiding-intentions

Pollux, A. (n.d.). *The Ultimate Full Moon Money Spell for Abundance.* Welcome To Wicca Now. Retrieved from https://wiccanow.com/full-moon-money-spell/

Bacon, Roger (1659, London). His Discovery of the Miracles of Art, Nature, and Magic. Faithfully translated out of Dr. Dees own Copy, by T. M. and never before in English.

Crowley, Aleister (1979), The Confessions of Aleister Crowley, Routledge & Kegan Paul

Crowley, Aleister (1985), Eight Lectures on Yoga, Falcon Press
Crowley, Aleister (1974), The Equinox of the Gods, Gordon Press
Crowley, Aleister (1997), Magic (Book 4), Weiser
Crowley, Aleister (1973), Magic Without Tears, Falcon Press